REFRIGE AND AIR CONDITION TECHNICIAN FIRST YEAR MCQ

OBJECTIVE QUESTION ANSWERS

MANOJ DOLE

Copyright © Manoj Dole
All Rights Reserved.

This book has been published with all efforts taken to make the material error-free after the consent of the author. However, the author and the publisher do not assume and hereby disclaim any liability to any party for any loss, damage, or disruption caused by errors or omissions, whether such errors or omissions result from negligence, accident, or any other cause.

While every effort has been made to avoid any mistake or omission, this publication is being sold on the condition and understanding that neither the author nor the publishers or printers would be liable in any manner to any person by reason of any mistake or omission in this publication or for any action taken or omitted to be taken or advice rendered or accepted on the basis of this work. For any defect in printing or binding the publishers will be liable only to replace the defective copy by another copy of this work then available.

Digitization is the need of the time. In the future, training in industrial training institutes will need to be conducted using online internet to make training more convenient and easy. E-books containing a set of MCQ questions will be made available to the trainees as they need to be more accustomed to the multiple choice questions MCQ to prepare for the online exams taking place in their industrial training institutes.

With all these factors in mind, Mr. Manoj Madhukar Dole Instructor, Industrial Training Institute, Satara, has written books according to the new annual system and NSQF-5 syllabus. And they've created theoretical mobile apps and blogs to make training easier, and made all these educational materials available for download on the world famous websites Google Play Store, Amazon and Apple Book Store.

The books were published by Hon'ble Joint Director Shri Rajendra Ghume Saheb Regional Office of Vocational Education and Training, Pune on 9/1/2019, at this time Shri Prakash Saigavkar Saheb Principal Government Industrial Training Institute Aundh Pune, Shri Tukaram Misal Saheb Principal Govt. Q. Sanstha Satara, Shri Sachin Dhumal Saheb District Vocational Education and Training Officer Satara, Shri Yatin Pargaonkar Saheb Principal Govt. Q. Sanstha Kolhapur, Shri Vikas Teke Saheb Inspector Vocational Education and Training Regional Office Pune, Palekar Foods Products Pvt. Ltd. Entrepreneurial Chairman of Satara Mr. Nilkanthrao Palekar Saheb, Chairman of Hira Foods Mr. Ibrahim Baba Tamboli Saheb, Mrs. Shalmali Pawar Headmaster Government Technical School Center Satara and other dignitaries were present on the occasion.

Contents

Prologue .... *vii*

Foreword .... *ix*

Preface .... *xi*

Acknowledgements .... *xiii*

1. Refrigeration And Air Condition Technician First Year Mcq Drawing 1

2. Refrigeration And Air Condition Technician First Year Mcq 26

Prologue

Refrigeration and Air Condition Technician First Year MCQ is a simple Book for ITI Course Revised NSQ F-5 Syllabus, It contains objective questions with underlined & bold correct answers MCQ covering all topics including all about the latest & Important about safety precautions, marking, sawing, filing, drilling, reaming, taping and dieing etc.

Produce Sheet metal components Identify electrical safety. Join different wire, measure power, currents, volts and earth resistance etc. Connect single phase, 3 phase motors i.e. star and delta connections. Identify the electronic components and their colour code i.e. transistor, capacitor, diode, amplifier, I.C and able to work soldering. Perform gas welding, brazing, soldering observing related safety. Identify RAC tools and equipment and recognize different parts of RAC system. Perform copper tube cutting, flaring, swaging, brazing. Test mechanical & electrical components. Perform leak test, vacuuming, gas charging, wiring & installation of refrigerator.

Perform door alignment, door gasket fitting, replace door switch. Test compressor motor terminal, start compressor Direct with relay & without relay, technique of flushing, leak testing, replacing capillary & filter drier, evacuation & gas charging. Check components of frost-free refrigerator (electrical / mechanical), wiring of frost-free freeze & air distribution in refrigerator sector. Leak detection, evacuators & gas charging. Dismantle, repair and assemble hermetic, fixed and variable speed compressor, and test performance. Identify the terminals of sealed compressor and their wiring and measure current, volts, watts and use of DOL starter with different types of motors Perform selection of Hermetic compressor for different appliances, starting methods, testing controls & safety cut out used in sealed compressor. Identify the components of control system of Inverter A.C and wiring of control systemPerform servicing & de-scaling of condenser (internals &externals) used in different appliances

Perform fitting & adjustment of drier, filter & refrigerant controls used in different refrigeration system.Perform servicing of different evaporator used in different appliances.Carry out Recovery and Recycling of Refrigerant used, alternative of CFC, HFC re-cover, transfer & handling of gas cylinders.Retrofit CFC/HFC machine with ozone friendly refrigerant with understanding of the compatibility.Pack thermal insulation and prevent cooling leakage.

Install window AC, test Electrical & electronics components & Fault diagnosis & remedial measures.Perform servicing of electrical & electronic control test, installation, wiring, fault finding & remedial measures of different split AC.Perform servicing of car AC. Fault diagnosis & remedial measures

We add new question answers with each new version. Please email us in case of any errors/omissions. This is arguably the largest and best e-Book for All engineering multiple choice questions and answers.

As a student you can use it for your exam prep. This e-Book is also useful for professors to refresh material.

Foreword

Vocational education and training is imparted through the Department of Vocational Education and Training through the Department of Business Education and Business Practical to supply multi-skilled artisans in line with the rapidly growing demand in the industrial sector in the 21st century. All the occupations within the institutions are important, as the trainees from these occupations develop multi-skills as per the demands of the industry.

with the noble intention of making available MCQ e-books suitable for all businesses, considering that all the examinations in all the industries in the industrial sector are conducted online and include MCQ method questions. Mr. Manoj Madhukar Dole has written a very good e-book on MCQ method as per the new annual syllabus. This e-book will definitely be a guide for all the trainees, trainee candidates, training instructors and others concerned.

The author of the book is Mr. Manoj Madhukar Dole, Instructor Gov. ITI Satara has 17 years of training experience. Written as a new annual pattern, this e-book incorporates modern digital QR Code technology to understand the layout, simple language, and simple syntax, diagrams and videos for each subject. So I am sure that this e-book will definitely be useful for in-depth study and exam practice. The work they have done is certainly commendable.

Mr. Tukaram Misal
Principal Government Industrial Training Institute Satara.

Preface

DGET New Delhi and CSTARI Kolkata have been implementing an annual pattern for all businesses in ITI since the August 2018 session. The examination system will also be changed and it will be online from this year and since all the questions are of Objective Type (MCQ), the trainees are in dire need of in-depth study. It is with this in mind that we are delighted to present the books based on the old NIMI pattern and a complete overview of the new annual pattern, and we hope that these books will be a guide for all business directors and trainees. Is.

For writing these books, Johar Awate Saheb, Principal of ITI Akluj. Former Principal of ITI Satara Saigavkar Saheb, Assistant Director Shri Chandrakant Dhekne Saheb Regional Office of Vocational Education and Training, Pune, District Vocational Education and Training Officer Sachin Dhumal Saheb and Headmaster Government Technical School Kendra Shalmali Pawar Madam and son Adhiraj Dole, mother Kusum Dole, I am very grateful to my father Madhukar Dole and wife Ashwini Dole for their special guidance and cooperation from time to time.

Also, in a very short period of time, the book was reviewed by Shri Rajendra Ghume Saheb, Joint Director, Vocational Education and Training Regional Office, Pune, for his invaluable time in publishing the book. I am sincerely grateful for their feedback.

I am grateful to the Instructor of ITI Satara for there continuous support from the very beginning of writing the book.

From this book, I consider myself blessed to have shared my thoughts on e-learning with you. I will not claim that this book is perfect, because considering the perfection, this book is an attempt and is in its infancy. They will be valuable for improvement if they are tested and suggested.

Manoj Dole
Dated 9/1/2019

Acknowledgements

The industrial training and theoretical examination system of our industrial training institutes and these changes have been accepted by the craft instructors and the trainees. Theoretical examinations conducted in your industrial training institutes are also conducted online. Since these examinations are of multiple choice MCQ method, the trainees will need to get more practice of such questions.

With all these considerations in mind, Mr. Manoj Madhukar, Director, Dole Crafts, Katari Industrial Training Institute, Satara, has done a thorough study and with his diligent work and added his keen intellect, according to the new annual system and NSQF-5 syllabus, e-book of Katari and other machine trades. -Book) and they have created mobile apps and blogs on theoretical topics to make training easier and have made all these educational materials available for download on the world famous websites Google Play Store, Amazon and Apple Book Store. Training has been made easier by creating a print version and using advanced techniques like QR Code.

All these educational materials will definitely be a guide for all the trainees for in-depth study and for the craft instructors and other concerned who are imparting vocational training.

CHAPTER ONE

Refrigeration and Air Condition Technician First Year MCQ Drawing

REFRIGERATION AND AIR CONDITION TECHNICIAN FIRST YEAR MCQ

Fire extinguisher

Calliper

REFRIGERATION AND AIR CONDITION TECHNICIAN FIRST YEAR MCQ

Hacksaw frame

Universal surface guage

Hammer

Centre punch

Bench vice

Files

REFRIGERATION AND AIR CONDITION TECHNICIAN FIRST YEAR MCQ

Scraper

Surface Plate

Outside Micrometer

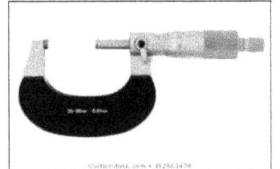 

Micrometer

Depth micrometer

Vernier Calliper

Vernier bevel protractor

Drilling

Reamer

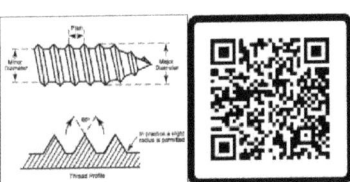
Thread

Tap Die

Grinding Wheel

Tap Die

Centre gauge

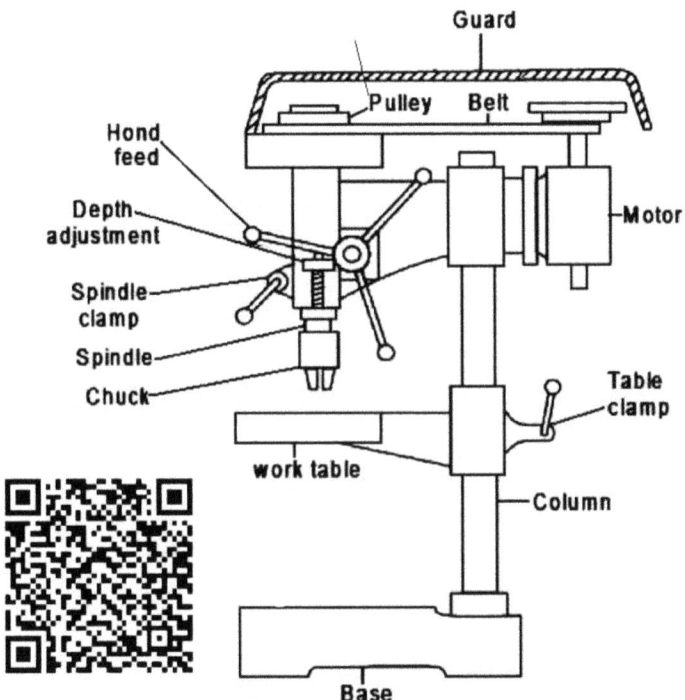

Piller Drilling Machine

REFRIGERATION AND AIR CONDITION TECHNICIAN FIRST YEAR MCQ

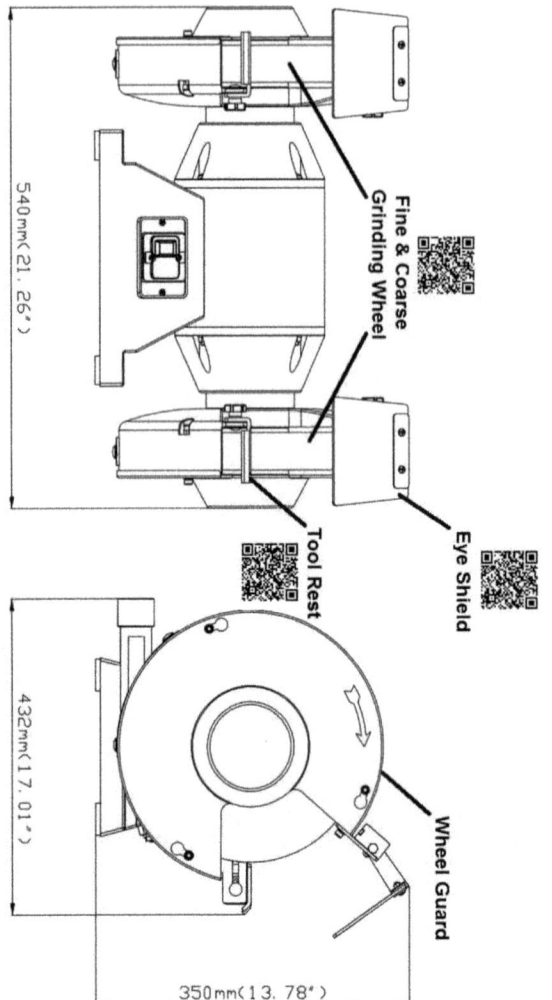

Sheet Metal Tools

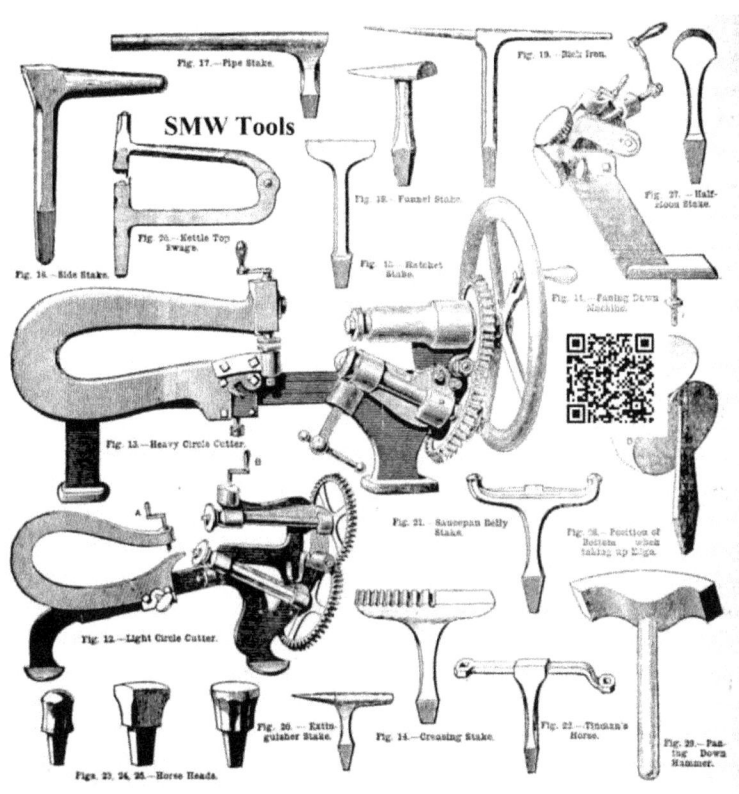

REFRIGERATION AND AIR CONDITION TECHNICIAN FIRST YEAR MCQ

multimeter

ohmmeter

resistores

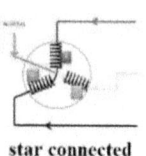 
star connected alternator

voltmeter ammeter

wattmeter

• 16 •

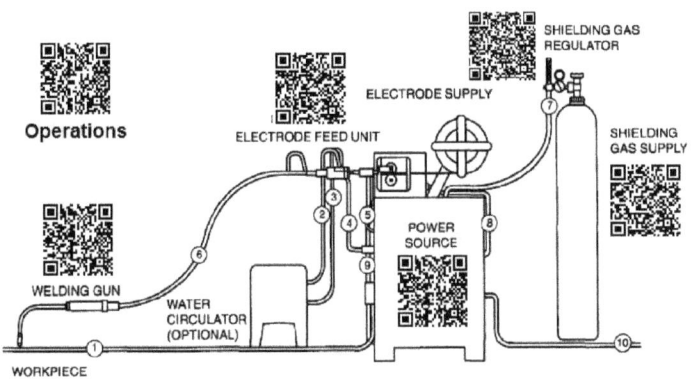

Gas Metal Arc Welding

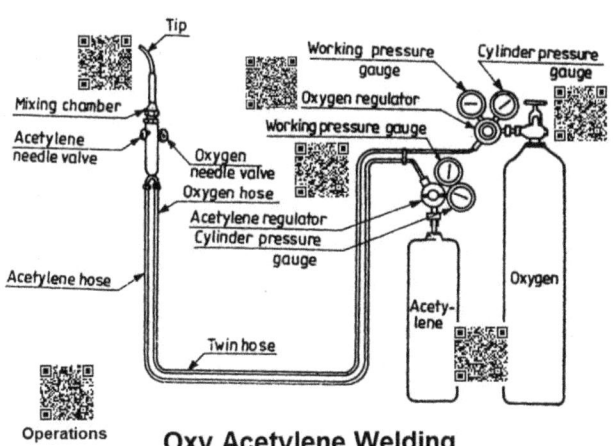

Oxy Acetylene Welding

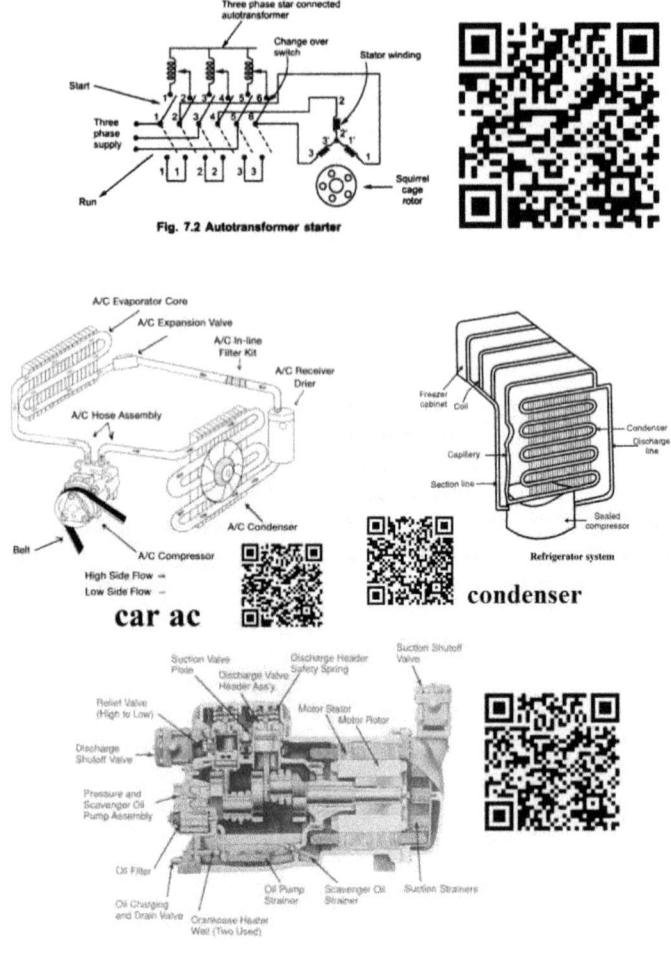

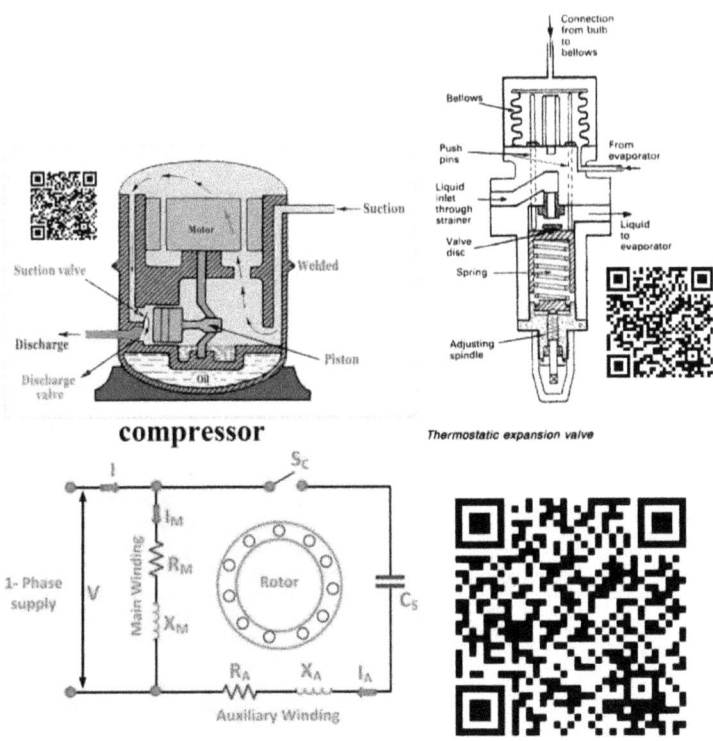

compressor

Thermostatic expansion valve

CSIR motor

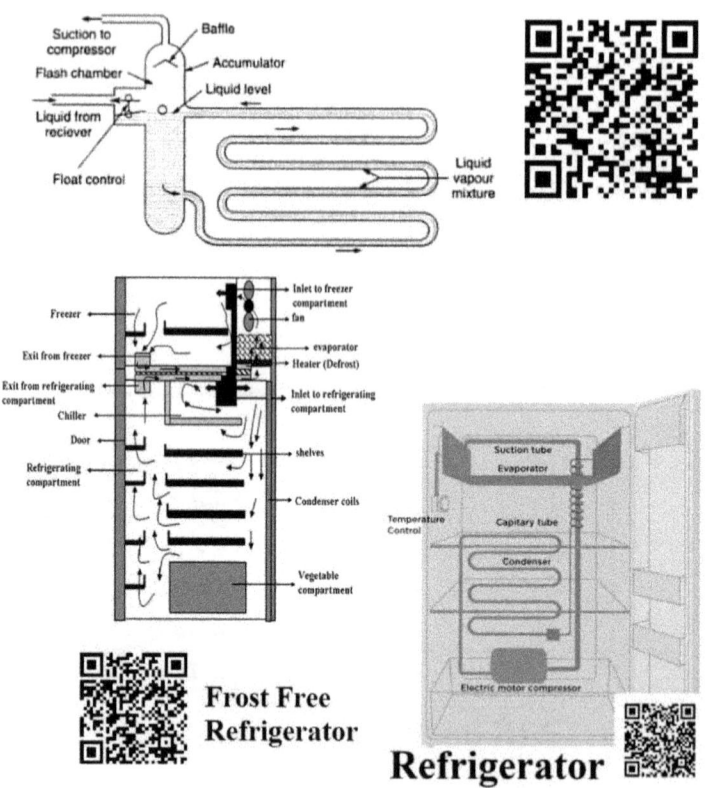

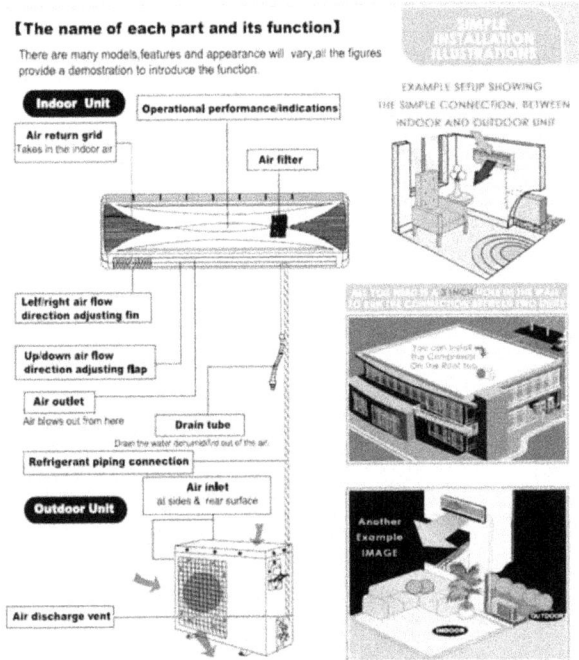

inverter split ac

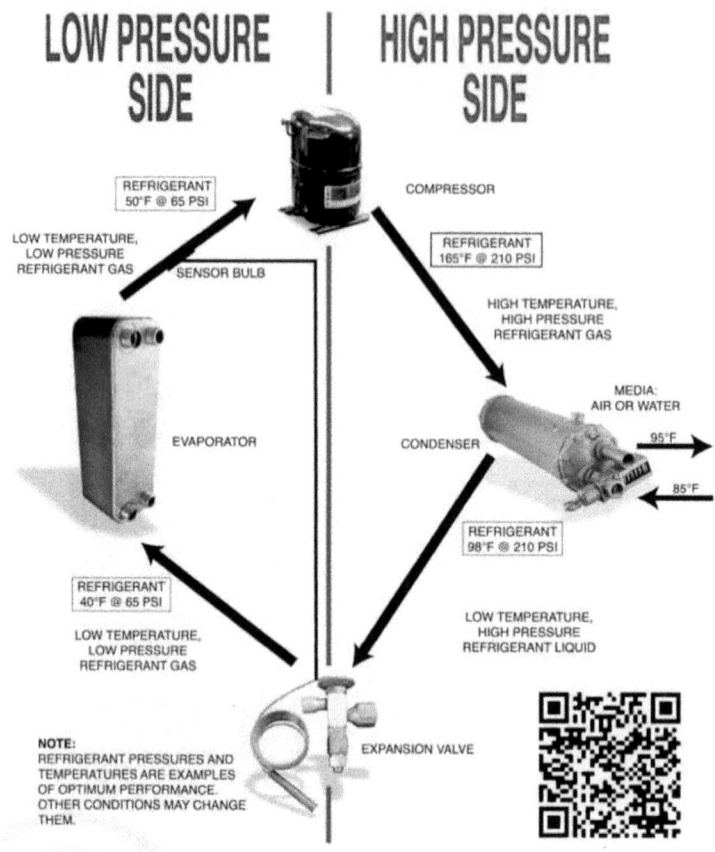

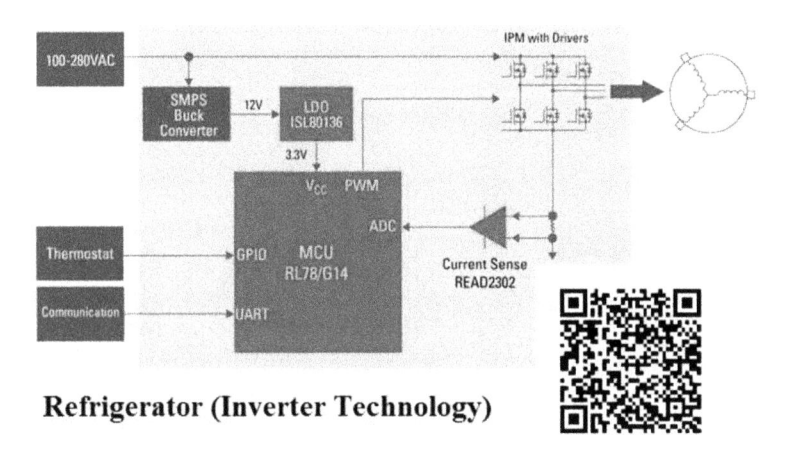

Refrigerator (Inverter Technology)

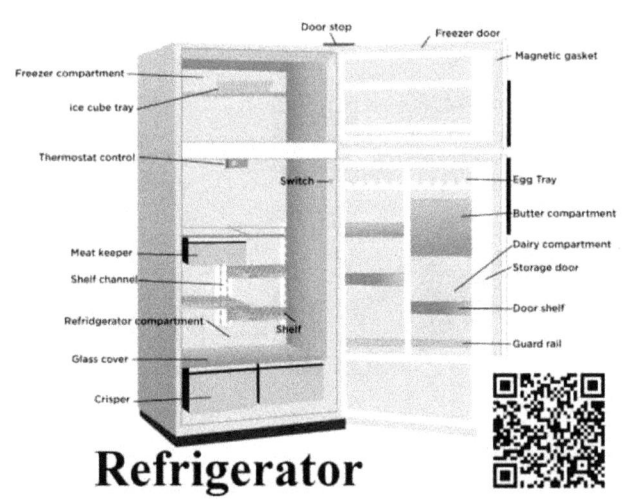

Refrigerator

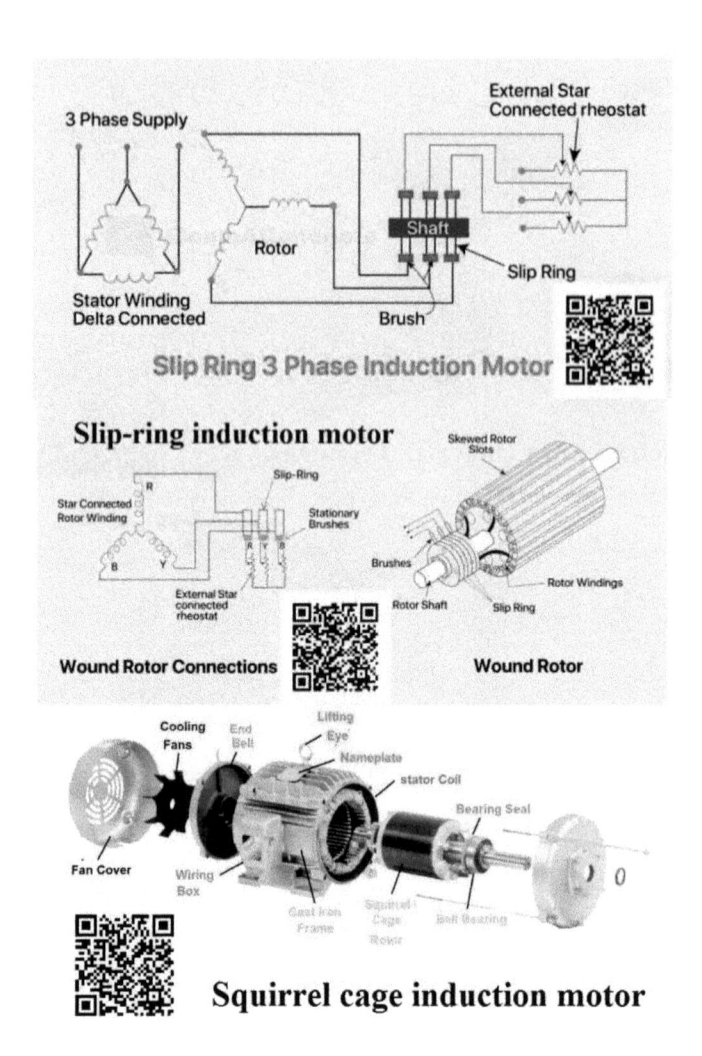

REFRIGERATION AND AIR CONDITION TECHNICIAN FIRST YEAR MCQ

Slip Ring 3 Phase Induction Motor

Slip-ring induction motor

Squirrel cage induction motor

Vapour Compression Refrigeration System

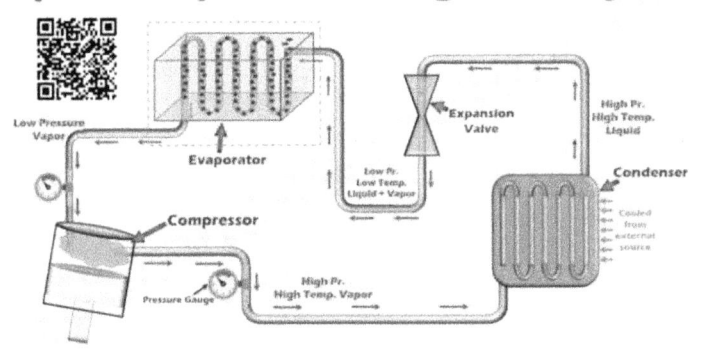

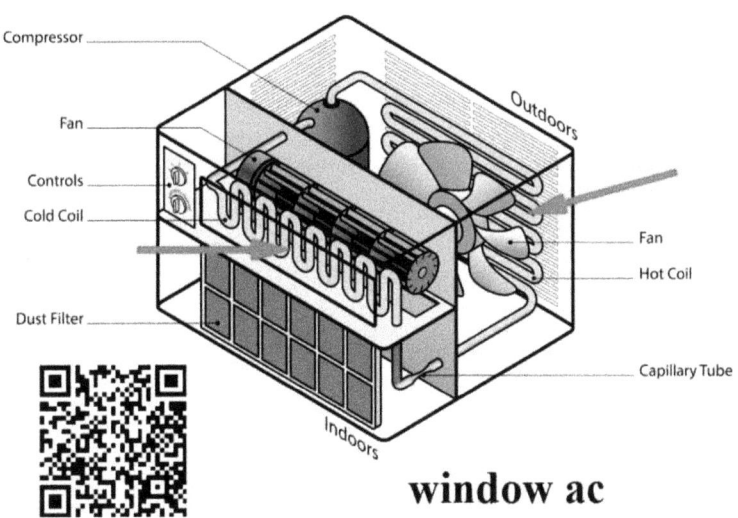

window ac

CHAPTER TWO

Refrigeration and Air Condition Technician First Year MCQ

1] Which one is a workshop safety?
   <u>A] Keep shop floor clean and free from grease, oil or other slippery materials</u>
   B] Stop the machine before changing the speed
   C] Don't use cracked or chipped tools
   D] Don't try to stop a running machine with hand
2] In Personal Protect Equipment (PPE) HELMET is used to
<u>A] protect head</u>
B] Protect eyes
C] Protect hands
D] Protect ears
3] Which of the following belongs to general safety?
A Have a worker in good attitude
B] The work clean and clear
C] Concentrate on your work
<u>D] Keep the floor and gangways clean and clear</u>
4] While grinding, which is used to protect the eyes?
A] Dark green glass
B] Mask
C] Sun glasses
<u>D] Safety goggles</u>
5] Which of the following is done for machine safety?
<u>A] Check the oil level before starting the machine</u>

B] Do things in a methodical way
C] Keep the floor and gangways clean and clear
D] Don't use dies and scarves

6] In Personal Protect Equipment (PPE], 'sleeves' is used to protect ----------

A] Face
B] Eyes
C] Ears
D] Hands

7] ABC stands for --------------
A] Automatic Breathing Control
B] Automatic Blood Control
C] Airway Breathing Circulation
D] Automatic Blood Circulation

8] Fire & FIRE EXTINGUISHERS

Fire extinguisher

9] To put off "Class B" fire, the types of fire extinguisher used is ....
A] dry power
B] Carbon dioxide
C] Jet of water
D] Foam type

10] Which type of fire extinguisher is used to put off general fire?
A] Water type Extinguisher
B] Foam type Extinguisher
C] Dry chemical powder Extinguisher
D] Carbon dioxide (C02] Extinguisher

11] In case of bleeding, take treatment Of
D] cold 3" and rest
A] spray cold water
B] Bandage immediately -----.

B] Enquire about the accident thought treatment

12] in case of an accident, the victim should im
A] Asked to take rest
C] Attended immediately
D] leave him
13] First aid is given to an injured or ill person primarily....
A] Save life
B] Prevent further deterioration of the muff's
C] Give best possible comfort
D] All of these
14] Colour code for Bins for waste paper segregation is -----
A] blue Colour
B] Yellow Colour
C] Red Colour
D] Green Colour
15] In Japanese Seiko stands for --------------
A] Shine
B] Sort
C] Standardize
D] Sustain
16] Benefit of SS system is ------
A] Increase in productivity
B] Increase in quality
C] Reduction in wastage of time
D] All of these
17] Safety is -----------
A] nobody's business
B] every bodise business
C] Some bodies business
D] The organization business

18] For basic categories of safety signs are available The meaning of "prohibition" sign ----
A] shows it must not be done
B] Shows what must be done
C] Warns the hazard or danger
D] Gives information of safety provision

18] One micrometer (U) is equal to...
A] 0.1mm
B] 0.01mm
C] 0.001mm
D] 0.0001mm

19] The caliper meant for measuring the width of a slot is...
A] Odd leg caliper
B] Outside caliper
C] Jenny caliper
D] Inside calliper

Calliper

20] The size of the dividers are specified by the ----------
A] Total length of legs
B] Distance between the points when fully opened
C] Length of legs without points
D] distance between the pivot and the point

21] The instrument used to mark parallel lines, parallel to the datum edge is -
A] jenny caliper
B] Divider
C] Outside calliper
D] Inside calliper

22] Which one of the following is an indirect measuring tool?
A] Outside caliper

B] Vernier calliper
C] Steel rule
D] Outside micrometer

23] For cutting thin tubing, the most suitable pitch of the hacksaw blade is...
A] 1.8mm
B] 1.4mm
C] 1mm
D] <u>0.8mm</u>

24] For cutting solid brass, the most suitable pitch of the hacksaw blade is...
A] <u>1.8mm</u>
B] 1.4mm
C] 1mm
D] 0.8mm

Hacksaw frame

25] A new hacksaw blade after a few strokes becomes loose because of the...
A] <u>Stretching of the blade</u>
B] Wing-nut threads being worn out
C] Wrong pitch of the blade
D] Improper selection of the set of saws.

26] While cutting small diameter pipes, it is advisable to watch regularly and ensure that...
A] The cut is along the curved line
B] <u>More saw teeth are in contract</u>
C] The work is not overheated
D] Proper balancing of hacksaw is maintained

27] The vice clamps are used to...

A] Protect hard jaws
B] Clamp the work pieces rigidly
C] <u>Protect the finished surfaces</u>
D] Prevent the movable jaw being filed

28] The reference surface during marking is provided by the...
A] Surface gauge
B] Workpiece
C] Drawing of the work
D] <u>Marking table surface</u>

29] The size of an engineer's vice is specified by the...
A] Length of the movable jaw
B] <u>Width of the jaws</u>
C] Height of the vice
D] Maximum opening of the jaws

30] The part of the universal surface gauge which helps to draw a parallel line along a datum edge is the..
A] Rocker arm
B] Snug
C] Fine adjustment screw
D] <u>Guide pins</u>

Universal surface guage

31] Scribers are made of...
A] Mild steel
B] <u>High carbon steel</u>
C] Brass
D] Cast iron

32] Portion of the hammer used for fixing the handle is...
A] Face
B] Peen
C] Cheek
D] <u>Eye hole</u>

33] Weight of the hammer for the marking purpose is...
A] <u>250g</u>
B] 500g
C] 1 kg
D] 2 kgs

Hammer

34] The size of the dividers are specified by the...
A] Total length of the legs
B] Distance between the points when fully opened
C] Length of legs without the points
D] <u>Distance between the pivot and the point</u>

35] The included angle of the groove of 'V' block is always....
A] 45°
B] 60°
C] 90°
D] <u>120°</u>

36] 'V' blocks are available in grades of...
A] <u>A & B</u>
B] A,B & C
C] 1,2 & 3
D] 1 & 2

37] 'V' blocks of grade 'B' are made of
A] <u>Cast iron</u>

B] Mild steel
C] Steel
D] Cast steel
38] Name the punch used to locate the centre.
A] Prick punch 30°
B] Prick punch 60°
C] Centre punch
D] Dot punch

Centre punch

39] The point angle of centre punch is --------
A] 30°
B] 50°
c] 900
D] 1200
40] Punches are used for forming ---------of any shape
A] Holes
B] Mining
C] Knurling
D] Reaming
41] Generally the length of the handle of the vice is ----------
A] 1.5 times the normal size of the vice
B] 2.5 times the normal size of the vice
C] 3.5 times the normal size of the vice
D] 4.5 times the normal size of the vice

Bench vice

42] Bench vice spindle is made of ....
A] mild steel
B] Cast iron
C] Tool steel
D] Bronze

43] The convexity of files helps...
A] To file concave surfaces
B] To file convex surfaces
C] To prevent rounding of edges of work
D] The file to become straight when pressure is applied

Files

44] Which file used for filling wood, leather and other soft material? .
A] Single cut file
B] Double cut file
c] Rasp cut file
D] Curved cut file

45] File used is used for ------------
A] Cleaning the work piece

C] Renewing the file teeth
B] cleaning the file teeth
D] Cleaning the chips
46] File card is used to --------
A] Clean the work piece
C] Renew the file teeth
B] Clean the file teeth
47] The point angle of scriber is ----------
A] 30°
B] 60°
C] 5° to 10°
D] 12° to 15°
48] The cutting angle for chipping cast iron is...
A] 37.5°
B] 55°
C] 60°
D] 90°

49] The chisel will dig into the material when...
A] The rake angle is more
B] The clearance angle is too low
C] The angle of inclination is more
D] The angle of inclination is too low
50] A slight convexity is given to the cutting edge to...
A] Cut curved surfaces
B] Cut sharp corners
C] Prevent digging of the ends
D] Allow the lubricant to enter
51] Surface plates are made of...
A] High grade cast steel
B] Fine-grained cast iron
C] Alloy steels

D] Wrought iron

52] Surface plates are specified by their length and breadth & are in
A] decimetre
B] Cubic meter
C] Cylindrical
53] Ribs are given on the unmachined portion of the angle plate for...
A] Easy handling
B] Convenience in manufacturing
C] Clamping while setting on machines
D] Rigidity and to prevent distortion
54] The slots on the angle plate are given for...
A] Reducing weight
B] Aligning the work
C] Lifting using hooks
D] Accommodating bolts.
55] The size of the angle plates is stated by...
A] Weight
B] Length
C] Length x width
D] Size number
56] for high speed parting off work on material like cemented carbide Is'
A] Do all machine
B] Cutting off machine
C] Heavy duty power saw
D] Mining machine sitting saw
57] Gun metal is an alloy of copper, ------------
A] tin and zinc
B] Lead and zinc
C] Zinc and nickel
D] Lead and nickel
58] Cast iron is used for manufacturing machine beds because -------

A] it can resist more compressive stress
B] it is heavy in weight
C] It is cheaper metal
D] It is a brittle metal

59] Accuracy or least count of a metric outside micrometric is ---------
A] 0-1 mm
B] 0.01 mm
C] 0.001 mm
D] 0.02 mm

60] 1000 microns means -----
A] 1 mm
B] 1 m
C] 1000 mm
D] 10 cm

61] in a metric micrometer, a complete revolution of thimble advances
A] 0.01 mm
B] 0.25 mm
C] 0.50 mm
D] 1.00mm

Micrometer

62] Ratchet Stop in the micrometer helps to ------------
A] Control the pressure
B] lock the spindle
C] Adjust the zero error
D] Hold the work piece

63] 1000 micron means ------------
A] 1 mm
B] 1 m
C] 1000 mm
D] 10 cm

64] What is the zero reading of a 50-75 mm outside micrometer?
A] 0.000 mm
B] 0.01 mm
C] 25.00 mm
D] 50.00 mm

65] The value of the smallest division on sleeve of a metric outside micrometer is -----
A] 0.50 mm
B] 1.00 mm
C] 1.50 mm
D] 2.00 mm

66] Ratchet stop in the micrometer helps to ---------
A] control the pressure
B] Lock the spindle
C] Adjust the zero error
D] Hold the work piece

67] Least count of depth micrometer is
A] 0.5 mm
B] 0.2 mm
C] 0.001 mm
D] 0.01 mm

Depth micrometer

68] The least count of vernier calliper is (main scale = 49 division, vernier scale = 50 division]
A] 0.1 mm
B] 0.01 mm
C] 0.001 mm
D] 0.02 mm

Vernier Calliper

69] The type of measurement made by using a Vernier Calliper is -------
A] Direct measurement
B] Indirect measurement
C] 90"] (a] 81 (b]
D] None of these

76] The taper shank drills are held on the machine by means of...
A] Chucks
B] Sleeves
C] Drift
D] Vice

77] Drill chucks are fitted on the drilling machine spindle by means of a...
   A] Knurled ring
   B] Arbor
   C] Drift
   D] Pinion and key

78] The Morse taper provided on drills ranges between...
   A] MT 1 to MT 5
   B] MT 1 to MT 4
   C] MT 0 to MT 5
   D] MT 0 to MT 4

79] A drift is used for...
   A] Drawing a drill location
   B] Fixing chuck on the machine spindle
   C] Removing a broken drill from the work
   D] Removing the drill from the machine spindle

80] When the taper shank of the drill is larger than the machine spindle, the device to hold the drill is a...
   A] Drill sleeve
   B] Taper socket
   C] Drill drift
   D] Chuck and key

81] The suitable cutting fluid for drilling mild steel in a drilling machine is...
   A] Synthetic soluble oil
   B] Neat oil
   C] Distilled water
   D] Soluble oil

82] A special feature of the radial drilling machine is...
   A] It can be used for drilling with a H.S.S. drill
   B] Table can be moved and set at any position
   C] A variety of speeds is available
   D] The spindle can be brought to any position

83] The point angle of drills depends on...
A] The size of the drill
B] The type of machine
C] The material of the work
D] The RPM of the drill
84] The point angle for a standard drill is...
A] 60°
B] 108°
C] 118°
D] 135°
85] The helical angle determines the...
A] Cutting angle
B] Chew angle
C] Rake angle
D] Lip angle
86] The clearance angle of the drill is between...
A] 3° to 5°
B] 8° to 12°
C] 12° to 20°
D] 15° to 20°
87] In a remote place (no electricity available] a rail track is to be drilled. Choose the right drilling machine
A] Radial drilling machine
B] Pillar drilling machine
C] Ratchet drilling machine
D] Sensitive drilling Machine

Drilling
88] A drilling machine used by a carpenter for cabinet making is a...
A] Ratchet drilling machine
B] Radial drilling machine
C] <u>Breast drilling machine</u>
D] Sensitive drilling machine
89] Which one of the following drilling machines is used for drilling holes where electricity is not available?
A] Bench drilling machine
B] Pillar drilling machine
C] Redial drilling machine
D] <u>Ratchet drilling machine</u>
90] Which one of the following drilling machine is used for heavy duty work?
A] Bench drilling machine
B] Pillar drilling machine
C] <u>Radial drilling machine</u>
D] Electric hand drilling machine
91] Drill chuck are held on the machine spindle by means of ------
A] <u>arbor</u>
B] Drift
C] draw-in bar
D] Chuck nut
92] Different speeds are obtained in a sensitive bench drilling machine by ----
A] <u>Belt pulley mechanism</u>
B] Hydraulic mechanism
C] Rack and Pinion mechanism
D] Cam and follower mechanism

Q 1. _____ is used as a longitudinal corner seam for various types of pipes such as duct work.
A). Grooved seam
B). <u>Pittsburgh seam</u>
C). Dovetail seam
D). Pane down seam

Q 2. The hand groover is made up of _____ and is used to make_____ grooved joint.
A). cast steel, internal locked
B). cast iron, external locked
C). <u>cast steel, external locked</u>
D). cast iron, internal locked

Q 3. Which of the following is not an advantage of false wiring
A). Cost of the article is reduced
B). Weight of the article is reduced
C). It helps to maintain the sides in position
D). <u>Weight of the article is increased</u>

Q 4. The stretchout of a round pipe is the_____ of the pipe.
A). Area
B). <u>circumference</u>
C). diameter
D). radius

Q 6. Identify the component X of Hand lever punch as shown in figure
A). Die
B). Punch holder
C). <u>Throat</u>
D). Gauge

Q 7. Formula generally used in the shop floor for determining the length of snap head rivet is - (where L=shank length, T=total thickness of the number of plates used and D= rivet diameter)
A). <u>L=T+1.5D</u>
B). L=T+0.6D
C). L=T+2.5D
D). L=T+2D

Q 8. Which clip is generally used for connecting cross seams on ducts
A). Government clip
B). <u>Drive clip</u>
C). Nailing clip

D). S clip S

Q 9. Identify the type of self tapping screw as shown in figure
A). <u>Type-A</u>
B). Type-B
C). Type-C
D). Type-D

Q 10. Which of the following is not a Semi-Permanent Treatmen
A). Galvanising
B). Tinning
C). Cladding
D). <u>Anodising</u>

Q 11. _____ is used to provide a decorative and corrosion resistant coating on aluminium and its alloys only.
A). Electroplating
B). <u>Anodising</u>
C). Cladding
D). Galvanising

Q 12. _____ is used for scribing circles, arcs and for transforming and stepping off distances.
A). Trammel
B). Radius gauge
C). <u>Wing compass</u>
D). Screw pitch gauge

Q 13. _____ is used for the internl side cutting of an intricated work. ____
A). Aviation shear
B). Bench shear
C). <u>Hawk Billed shear</u>
D). Double cutting shear

Q 14. Which of the following sheet metal hammer is used in raising operation
A). Riveting hammer
B). <u>Stretching hammer</u>
C). Creasing hammer
D). Planishing hammer

Q 15. Identify the type of spanner as shown in figure -
A). Ring spanner
B). Adjustable spanner

C). Socket spanner
D). Hook spanner
Q 17. _____ is used for drilling small diameter holes upto 6 mm.
A). Bevel gear type drilling machine
B). Ratchet drilling machine
C). Breast drilling machine
D). None of these
Q 18. Identify the drilling machine as shown in figure
A). Bevel gear type drilling machine
B). Ratchet drilling machine
C). Breast drilling machine
D). Pneumatic hand drilling machine
Q 21. Identify the component no. 6 of Universal swaging machine as shown in figure
A). Locking nut for rollers
B). Set of rollers
C). Upper shaft with gear
D). Lower shaft with gear
Q 22. _____ is used for forming the neck of a vessel after initial drawing. _____
A). Core die
B). Segmental die
C). Outside drawing die
D). Inside drawing die
Q 23. Identify the press as shown in figure
A). Straight side press
B). Pillar press
C). Adjustable bed press
D). Gap press
Q 24. _____ is the operation of forming the edge of an article into a roll. _____
A). Forming
B). Curling
C). Plunging
D). Cupping
Q 25. Which of the following is not a method of Polishing a metal by machine

A). <u>Polishing with pedestal grinder</u>
B). Polishing with compounds and cloth wheels
C). Polishing with abrasive covered wheels
D). Polishing with coated abrasive

Q 26. Which of the following buffing material is a powdered lava, white in colour used for scrubbing, cleaning and polishing
A). Tripoli
B). <u>Pumice</u>
C). Rouge
D). Whiting

Q 27. Identify the jig as shown in figure -
A). Solid jig
B). Post jig
C). <u>Trunnion jig</u>
D). Box jig

Q 28. In pipe bending machines, inner formers, lever, adjusting screw with lock nut and pipe guide are parts of _____
A). <u>Bench type hand operated pipe bender</u>
B). Portable hand operated pipe bender
C). Hydraulic bending machine
D). None of these

Q 30. Which type of welding is widely used in attaching fasteners to structural members
A). Spot welding
B). Seam welding
C). <u>Projection welding</u>
D). Flash butt welding

Q 31. Which of the following is not the equipment and accessories used for CO2 welding
A). Wire reel
B). Conduit linear
C). <u>Force mechanism</u>
D). Wire feed drive motor

Q 32. CO2 welding process cannot be used for welding _____.
A). silicon
B). aluminium
C). <u>zinc</u>
D). copper

Q 33. Which of the following is not the advantage of argon as shielding gas
A). Low arc voltage
B). Easy arc starting
C). Small heat affected zone
D). Low gas volume

Q 34. In air plasma cutting, _____ electrode is used where dry, clean compressed air is used as the cutting gas.
A). tungsten
B). argon
C). helium
D). zirconium

Q 35. In the coordinate system of AutoCAD 2008
A). Positive X figures are to the right
B). Positive X figures are to the left
C). Positive figures are in the direction vertically upwards
D). Positive figures are in the direction vertically downwards

Q 36. Water is used to extinguish_____.
A). Class-A fires
B). Class-B fires
C). Class-C fires
D). Class-D fires

Q 39. What is Galvanising
A). Process of coating zinc by hot dipping
B). Zinc diffusion process
C). Process used for making thin phosphate coating on steel
D). All of these

Q 40. Which seam is used in sheet metal joint for roofing and panelling
A). Double grooved seam
B). Lap seam
C). Double seam
D). Grooved seam

Q 41. A piece of material which is cut to the exact size and shape to form the desired object is called _____
A). Pattern
B). Templates
C). Stretchout
D). Development

Q 42. The term_____ refers to the sizes of flat piece of metal before it is formed into shape.
A). Stretchout
B). Free hand sketch
C). Actual size
D). Development of surface

Q 43. Which of the following is not possible with the parallel line method
A). Pyramid
B). Cube
C). Prism
D). Cylinder

Q 44. Which of the following is a method of dividing the surface of the object in traingles
A). Triangulation method
B). Geometrical construction methods
C). Parallel line method
D). Radial line method

Q 45. Which type of punches have hollow cross-section
A). Hollow punch
B). Solid punch
C). Number punch
D). Letter punch

Q 46. Which type of rivet is used in heavy structural work
A). Pan head rivet
B). Snap head rivet
C). Counter sunk rivet
D). Conical head rivet

Q 47. Identify the rivet as shown in figure
A). Pan head
B). Countersunk head
C). Snap head
D). Mushroom head

Q 48. The government clip are sometimes also called_____
A). Cup or Pocket Clip
B). Nailing Clip
C). Drive Clip
D). S-Clip

Q 49. Which clip is generally used for connecting cross seams on ducts
A). <u>Drive Clip</u>
B). S-Clip
C). Government Clip
D). Nailing Clip

Q 50. Which of the following solder is the alloy of copper, tin, silver, zinc, cadmium and phosphorus
A). <u>Hard solders</u>
B). Soft solders
C). Medium solders
D). Zinc solders

95] If the area of a metal wire of a given length is doubles, its resistance will...
A] be doubled
B] <u>be halved</u>
C] remain the same
D] be four times more

96].Among the following only one is regarded as resistance wire
A] gold
B] silver
C] <u>nichrome</u>
D] copper

97] Arc heating occurs when the air between electrodes of opposite polarity becomes..
A] moistened
B] dry
C] <u>ionized</u>
D] none of the above

98] The meter used to measure the temperature of furnace is...
A] hydrometer
B] <u>pyrometer</u>
C] hygrometer
D] tachometer

99] in the case of electrolyte a rise in temperature causes...
A] <u>decrease in resistance</u>
B] increase in resistance
C] no change in resistance
D] none of the above

100] Heat developed in a conductor is proportional to the...
A] square of the power
B] square of the resistance
C] **square of the current**
D] square of the time

101] Out of the four metal/alloys given below, one has almost no change in resistance for temperature change...
A] nickel
B] nichrome
C] platinum
D] **manganin**

102] A material that is slightly repelled by a magnet is called ...
A] magnetic
B] paramagnetic
C] **diamagnetic**
D] ferromagnetic

103] A material that can be magnetized only very slightly is called...
A] magnetic
B] **paramagnetic**
C] diamagnetic
D] ferromagnetic

104] Substances that can be magnetized easily and make very strong magnets are called...
A] **ferromagnetic**
B] diamagnetic
C] paramagnetic
D] permanent magnetic

105] A substance that has a high retentivity can be used for the manufacture of...
A] electromagnets
B] **permanent magnets**
C] temporary magnets
D] paramagnets

106] A substance that has low retentivity can be used for the manufacture of...
A] **electromagnets**
B] permanent magnets
C] bar magnets

D] paramagnets
107] The symbol for inductance is...
A] H
B] I
C] L
D] X
108] Tube lamp choke is the best example of...
A] open circuited
B] short circuited
C] grounded
D] connected to the neutral line
109] The initial function of a choke in a tube light circuit is to...
A] limit the starting current
B] induce high voltage
C] heat up the filament
D] limit the current after starting
110] The second function of a choke in a tube light circuit is to...
A] limit the starting current
B] induce high voltage
C] heat up the filament
D] limit the current after starting
111] The periodic time of a wave from is 2ms] Calculate the frequency
A] 50 HZ
B] 5 HZ
C] 500HZ
D] 5 KHZ
112] How big is the peak amplitude of a sine-wave with an effective value of 220 volts?
A] 311 V
B] 380 V
C] 400 V
D] 440 V
113] The peak-to-peak voltage is 99V] how big is the effective value of the sine wave?
A] 70 V
B] 44.5V
C] 49.5 V
D] 35 V

114] A moving coil voltmeter reads 10 V AC] How big is the effective voltage?
A] higher
B] lower
C] the same
D] 10% higher

115] A moving iron ammeter reads 10 A] how big is the peak current of the oscillation?
A] 7.07 A
B] 1.1414A
C] 70.7 A
D] 14.1 A

116] A current of 2 amps flows through a resistance of 10 ohms] The power dissipated in the resistance is equal to...
A] 20 watts
B] 200 watts
C] 40 watts
D] 5 watts

117] If the frequency changes from 50 HZ to 100 HZ keeping voltage constant, the inductive reactance of coil connected to supply...
A] remains same
B] become half
C] become doubled
D] become 4 times

118] Capacitance is not affected by...
A] plate area
B] distance between plates
C] dialectic material
D] frequency

119] The capacitive reactance of a capacitor varies...
A] directly with frequency
B] inversely with frequency
C] directly with applied voltage
D] inversely with applied voltage

120] A capacitor acquired 3 coulombs of charge when 6 volts are applied across it] It has a capacitance of ...
A] 0.5 farad
B] 3 farads

C] 3 farads
D] 18 farads

121] A capacitor is connected across a 200 volt AC line, its minimum voltage rating should be...
A] 100 volts
B] 200 Volts
C] <u>300 volts</u>
D] 400 volts

122] when testing a capacitor with an ohmmeter, the meter indicates some resistance] The capacitor under test is...
A] <u>leaky</u>
B] open
C] good
D] short

123] The total capacitance of a 40 micro farad capacitor connected in series with an 80 micro farad capacitor is...
A] <u>26.7 micro farad</u>
B] 40 micro farad
C] 60.6 micro farad
D] 120 micro farad

124] For obtaining 1 micro farad capacitor from 3 nos] of 3 micro farad capacitors we have to connect...
A] all in parallel
B] <u>all in series</u>
C] 2 series and one in parallel
D] none of the above

125] In an AC series circuit having R and C the current flowing through the capacitor will be...
A] lagging the voltage
B] <u>leading the voltage</u>
C] in phase with the voltage
D] none of the above

126] If the frequency of the supply is increased in the R-C series circuit the capacitive reactance will be
A] <u>reduced</u>
B] increased
C] having no effect
D] none of the above

127] Power companies are interested in improving the power factor to
A] reduce line current
B] increase motor efficiency
C] increase volt-amperes
D] decrease power

128] A capacitor increases the power factor value of an AC motor load when it is connected...
A] in series with the motor
B] in series with the starter
C] in parallel with the motor
D] in series with the main winding

129] Normally, the power factor of an incandescent lighting circuit is..
A] 0
B] 0.5
C] 0.707
D] 1.0

130] When resistance alone is used to determine current in an RLC series circuit, the circuit is...
A] an inductive circuit
B] a capacitive circuit
C] a combination circuit
D] a resonant circuit

131] Inductive reactance is directly related to..
A] resistance
B] frequency
C] capacitance
D] power

132] Synchronous motor when used for power factor improvement should be...
A] under excited
B] over excited
C] loaded
D] running at no load

133] In a RL parallel circuit, the opposition to total current is called...
A] reactance
B] resistance
C] a vector sum
D] impedance

134] In a AC parallel RL circuit, the power dissipated at the
A] impedance
B] resistance
C] inductance
D] capacitance

135] How much is the nominal output voltage of a carbon zinc cell?
A] 12V
B] 1.5V
C] 2.0V
D] 2.2V

136] Cells are connected in series to..
A] increase the output voltage
B] decreases the output voltage
C] decrease the internal resistance
D] increase the current capacity

54137connected in
A] series
B] parallel
C] series-parallel
D] parallel-series

138] The capacity of a cell is measured in
A] watt-hour
B] watts
C] amperes
D] ampere-hour

139] The primary cell which has the shortest shelf life is
A] carbon – zinc
B] alkaline
C] mercury
D] lithium

140] The cell which has very high energy density for given weight or volume to
A] carbon-zinc
B] alkaline
C] mercury
D] lithium

141] A 100-Ah capacity battery should deliver a current of 8A for approximately...

A] <u>12 h</u>
B] 8 h
C] 20 h
D] 100 h

142] When the battery is needed to be kept idle for a long time...
A] overcharge the battery
B] remove electrolyte
C] clean the plates with distilled water
D] <u>dry them and store the battery in cool dry clean place</u>

143] The active materials of the nickel iron cell are...
A] nickel hydroxide
B] powdered iron and its oxide
C] 21% solution of caustic potash
D] <u>all the above materials</u>

144] The capacity of a cell is measured in
A] watt hour
B] watts
C] amperes
D] <u>ampere-hour</u>

145] To charge a secondary cell, the system used is
A] low voltage AC
B] high voltage AC
C] AC
D] <u>DC</u>

146] What is the number of phases in a normal industrial supply system?
A] one
B] <u>three</u>
C] four
D] two

147] In a 3 phase star connected alternator, the coils have a phase difference of...
A] <u>120°</u>
B] 240°
C] 60°
D] 360°

148] Delta connection is used no one of the following
A] primary of the transmission line transformer
B] alternator winding

C] secondary of the distribution transformer
D] <u>primary of the distribution transformer</u>

149] Which method can be used to measure the power in a 3-phase unbalanced load system?
A] one wattmeter method
B] <u>tow wattmeter method</u>
C] three wattmeter method
D] three ammeter method

150] Two wattmeters can be used to measure 3-hase power in a 3-phase, 3 wire system with…
A] balanced load
B] unbalanced load
C] <u>balanced as well as unbalanced load</u>
D] out of balanced load

151] A single wattmeter can be used to measure power in a 3-phase system only when the load is..
A] <u>balanaced</u>
B] unbalanced
C] balanced as well as unbalanced load
D] constant

152] The force producing movement of the pointer in an indicating instrument is called as…
A] <u>deflecting force</u>
B] controlling force
C] damping force
D] distracting force

153] A permanent magnet moving coil instrument will read…
A] only AC quantities
B] <u>only DC quantities</u>
C] both AC and DC quantities
D] pulsating quantities

154] An instrument using gravity control will read correctly if used in..
A] <u>vertical position only</u>
B] horizontal position only
C] inclined position only
D] any position

155] Which one of the following damping methods is used in permanent magnet moving coil instrument?

A] air damping
B] fluid damping
C] spring damping
D] eddy current damping

156] Moving coil instrument works on the effect of...
A] chemical effect
B] heating effect
C] electrostatic effect
D] electromagnetic effect

157] The meter installed at your house to measure electrical energy is an example of...
A] indication type instrument
B] recording type instrument
C] indicating as well as recording type instrument
D] integrating type instrument

158].Which of the following material is preferred for permanent magnet?
A] alnico
B] y-alloy
C] silicon steel

1. A transistor has ....
A] one pn junction
B] two pn junctions
C] three pn junctions
D] four pn junctions

2. The number of depletion layers in a transistor is ....
A] four
B] three
C] one
D] two

3. The base of a transistor is .... doped
A] heavily
B] moderately
C] lightly
D] none of the above

4. The element that has the biggest size in a transistor is ....
A] collector
B] base

C] emitter
D] collector-base-junction
5. In a pnp transistor, the current carriers are ....
A] acceptor ions
B] donor ions
C] free electrons
D] <u>holes</u>
6. The collector of a transistor is .... doped
A] heavily
B] <u>moderately</u>
C] lightly
D] none of the above
7. A transistor is a .... operated device
A] <u>current</u>
B] voltage
C] both voltage and current
D] none of the above
8. In a npn transistor, ... are the minority carriers
A] free electrons
B] <u>holes</u>
C] donor ions
D] acceptor ions
9. The emitter of a transistor is .... doped
A] lightly
B] <u>heavily</u>
C] moderately
D] none of the above
10. In a transistor, the base current is about .... of emitter current
A] 25%
B] 20%
C] 35 %
D] <u>5%</u>
11. At the base-emitter junctions of a transistor, one finds ....
A] a reverse bias
B] a wide depletion layer
C] <u>low resistance</u>
D] none of the above
12. The input impedance of a transistor is ....

A] high
B] <u>low</u>
C] very high
D] almost zero

13. Most of the majority carriers from the emitter ....
A] recombine in the base
B] recombine in the emitter
C] <u>pass through the base region to the collector</u>
D] none of the above

14. The current IB is ....
A] <u>electron current</u>
B] hole current
C] donor ion current
D] acceptor ion current

15. In a transistor ....
A] IC = IE + IB
B] IB = IC + IE
C] IE = IC − IB
D] <u>IE = IC + IB</u>

16. The value of a of a transistor is ....
A] more than 1
B] <u>less than 1</u>
C] 1
D] none of the above

17. IC = aIE + ...
A] IB
B] ICEO
C] <u>ICBO</u>
D] ßIB

18. The output impedance of a transistor is ....
A] <u>high</u>
B] zero
C] low
D] very low

19. In a tansistor, IC = 100 mA and IE = 100.2 mA. The value of ß is ....
A] 100
B] 50

C] about 1
D] <u>200</u>
20. In a transistor if ß = 100 and collector current is 10 mA, then IE is ....
A] 100 mA
B] <u>100.1 mA</u>
C] 110 mA
D] none of the above
21. The relation between ß and a is ....
A] ß = 1 / (1 – a)
B] ß = (1 – a) / a
C] <u>ß = a / (1 – a)</u>
D] ß = a / (1 + a)
22. The value of ß for a transistor is generally ....
A] 1less than 1
B] between 20 and 500
C] <u>above 500</u>
23. The most commonly used transistor arrangement is .... arrangement
A] <u>common emitter</u>
B] common base
C] common collector
D] none of the above
24. The input impedance of a transistor connected in ....arrangement is the highest
A] common emitter
B] <u>common collector</u>
C] common base
D] none of the above
25. The output impedance of a transistor connected in ....
A] arrangement is the highest
B] common emitter
C] <u>common collector</u>
D] common base
none of the above
26. The phase difference between the input and output voltages in a common base arrangement is ....
A] 180o

B] 90o
C] 270o
D] <u>0o</u>

27. The power gain in a transistor connected in .... arrangement is the highest
A] <u>common emitter</u>
B] common base
C] common collector
D] none of the above

28. The phase difference between the input and output voltages of a transistor connected in common emitter arrangement is ....
A] 0o
B] <u>180o</u>
C] 90o
D] 270o

29. The voltage gain in a transistor connected in .... arrangement is the highest
A] common base
B] common collector
C] <u>common emitter</u>
D] none of the above

30. As the temperature of a transistor goes up, the base-emitter resistance ....
A] <u>decreases</u>
B] increases
C] remains the same
D] none of the above

31. The voltage gain of a transistor connected in common collector
A] arrangement is ....
B] equal to 1
C] more than 10
D] <u>more than 100 less than 1</u>

32. The phase difference between the input and output voltages of a transistor connected in common collector arrangement is ....
A] 180o
B] <u>0o</u>
C] 90o
D] 270o

33. IC = ß IB + ...
A] ICBO
B] IC
C] ICEO
D] aIE
34. IC = [a / (1 – a)] IB + ...
A] ICEO
B] ICBO
C] IC
D] (1 – a) IB
35. IC = [a / (1 – a)] IB + [........ / (1 – a)]
A] ICBO
B] ICEO
C] IC
D] IE
36. BC 147 transistor indicates that it is made of ....
A] germanium
B] silicon
C] carbon
D] none of the above
37. ICEO = (.........) ICBO
A] ß1
B] + a
C] 1 + ß
D] none of the above
38. A transistor is connected in CB mode. If it is not connected in CE mode with same bias voltages, the values of IE, IB and IC will ....
A] remain the same
B] increase
C] decrease
D] none of the above
39. If the value of a is 0.9, then value of ß is ....
A] 9
B] 0.9
C] 900
D] 90
40. In a transistor, signal is transferred from a .... circuit
A] high resistance to low resistance

B] <u>low resistance to high resistance</u>
C] high resistance to high resistance
D] low resistance to low resistance

41. The arrow in the symbol of a transistor indicates the direction of ....
A] electron current in the emitter
B] electron current in the collector
C] <u>hole current in the emitter</u>
D] donor ion current

42. The leakage current in CE arrangement is .... that in CB arrangement
A] <u>more than</u>
B] less than
C] the same as
D] none of the above

43. A heat sink is generally used with a transistor to ....
A] increase the forward current
B] decrease the forward current
C] compensate for excessive doping
D] <u>prevent excessive temperature rise</u>

44. The most commonly used semiconductor in the manufacture of a transistor is ....
A] germanium
B] <u>silicon</u>
C] carbon
D] none of the above

45. The collector-base junction in a transistor has ....
A] forward bias at all times
B] <u>reverse bias at all times</u>
C] low resistance
D] none of the above

40] The angle of below pipe to the line of weld in leftward welding technique is...
A] 40 to 50°
B] 50 to 60°
C] <u>60 to 70°</u>
D] 70 to 80°

41] The pressure of acetylene gas for gas cutting a 10mm M.S plate is...

A] <u>0.15 kgf/cm2</u>
B] 0.5 kgf/cm2
C] 1.0 kgf/cm2
D] 1.5 kgf/cm2

42] What size of the cutting nozzle you will select for cutting 10mm thick mild steel?
A] 0.8 mm
B] <u>1.2 mm</u>
C] 1.6 mm
D] 2.0 mm

43] The angle of filler rod in case of rightward welding technique is...
A] 10 to 20°
B] 20 to 30°
C] <u>30 to 40°</u>
D] 40 to 50°

44] One of the advantages of the high pressure system of gas welding is...
A] it is cheaper
B] <u>it is portable</u>
C] it is less dangerous
D] it does not require a skilled welder

45] Soldering of M.S sheets takes place at a temperature of...
A] 150°C
B] <u>250°C</u>
C] 400°C
D] 850°C

46] Forge welding is classified as...
A] fusion welding without pressure
B] <u>fusion welding with pressure</u>
C] non-fusion welding without pressure
D] no-fusion welding with pressure

47] The function of a gas regulator is...
A] get different types of flames
B] mix the gases in the required proportion
C] change the volume of gas flowing to the blow pipe
D] <u>set the working pressure</u>

48] For welding a lap fillet joint in vertical position by gas what should be the angle of below pipe to the line of weld?

A] 30° to 40°
B] 45°to 50°
C] 60° to 70°
D] 75° to 80°

49] Name the defect, in which the weld metal is flowing on to the surface of the base metal without fusing it
A] crater
B] overlap
C] lack of fusion
D] excessive convexity

50] What should be the angle of blow pipe between the two sheets while welding a T joint on 3.15mm M.S> sheet by gas welding?
A] 30°
B] 45°
C] 60°
D] 80°

51] Which metal pipe should NOT be used for passing acetylene gas in order to avoid explosions?
A] galvanized iron
B] stainless steel
C] mild steel
D] cooper

52] he percentage of carbon in acetylene gas is...
A] 99%
B] 92.3%
C] 89.1%
D] 85.3%

53] Acetylene gas contains
A] calcium, carbon and hydrogen
B] calcium and hydrogen
C] calcium, carbon, hydrogen and oxygen
D] carbon and hydrogen

54] In an acetylene purifier the sulphureted and phosphorated hydrogen are removed by...
A] pumice
B] water
C] filter wool

D] purifying chemicals
55].A hydraulic back pressure valve is used to...
A] increase the pressure of oxygen gas
B] increase the pressure of acetylene gas
C] prevent the danger of back fire
D] decrease the pressure of oxygen
56] The nozzle size required to weld a M.S pipe elbow joint with 3WT to get full depth fusion and good penetration is...
A] 5
B] 7
C] 10
D] 13
57] The selection of nozzle for pipe welding depends upon...
A] groove angle
B] welding position
C] pipe wall thickness
D] diameter of pipe
58] One of the functions of flux in gas welding is...
A] dissolve the metal oxides
B] reduce the melting point of mental
C] increase the flame temperature
D] increase the root penetration
59] The angle of vee groove of a single vee but joint for cast iron welding is...
A] 60°
B] 70°
C] 80°
D] 90°
60] On which of the following factors, the choice of flux for gas welding depend?
A] type of material to be joined
B] type of edge penetration
C] type of fuel gas
D] type of flame used
61].What is the nozzle size required to bronze weld 10mm thick cast iron job?
A] 5
B] 7

C] **10**
D] 13
62] State the suitable filler rod for bronze welding of cast iron
A] brass
B] **silicon bronze**
C] manganese bronze
D] super silicon cast iron
63] In bronze welding of cast iron, the base metal is heated upto a temperature of...
A] 300°C
B] **650°C**
C] 1000°C
D] 1300°C
64] Name the filler rod used for fusion welding of copper
A] manganese bronze rod
B] **copper silver alloy rod**
C] silicon bronze rod
D] pure copper rod
65] The divergence allowance required for gas welding a 300mm long copper butt joint is...
A] 1 to 2 mm
B] 2 to 3 mm
C] **3 to 4 mm**
D] 4 to 5 mm
66] The type of edge preparation done for gas welding a 4mm thick copper butt joint is...
A] single bevel
B] **single V**
C] double V
D] square
67] The nozzle size used for bronze welding of a 3.15 mm thick copper butt joint is...
A] 5
B] **7**
C] 10
D] 13
68] State the filler rod size required for welding a butt joint on 3mm thick brass sheet

A] 1.6 mm
B] 2 mm
C] 2.5 mm
D] <u>3 mm</u>

69] Name the weld defect which will occur if a No] 3 nozzle is used for welding a 3 mm thick brass sheet
A] undercut
B] burn through
C] porosity
D] <u>lack of penetration</u>

70] The size of nozzle used to gas weld 3.15 mm thick aluminium butt joint is...
A] 13
B] 10
C] 7
D] <u>5</u>

71] Nozzle size used for welding a 2 mm thick stainless steel sheet as a butt joint is...
A] 2
B] 3
C] 5
D] 7

72] What is the value of preheating temperature for gas welding of aluminium?
A] 100 to 120°C
B] <u>150 to 180°C</u>
C] 180 to 200°C
D] 210 to 250°C

73] In soldering operation the base metal is...
A] <u>not heated</u>
B] heated to 200°C
C] heated to 650°C
D] heated to red hot condition

74] For welding dissimilar metals, the following property of both the metals should not have wide variations
A] ductility
B] tensile strength

C] thermal expansion
D] wear resistance

75] Name the flux used for brazing of M.S] sheets
A] hydrochloric acid
B] zinc chloride
C] tallow resin
D] borax

76] In progressive gouging to what angle the gouging torch angle is reduced from the starting angle of 30°?
A] 20 to 25°
B] 15 to 20°
C] 10 to 15°
D] 5 to 10°

77] The thermit mixture used in thermit welding can be ignited with an initial temperature of..
A] 1500°C
B] 1200°C
C] 1000°C
D] 500°C

78] Shielded metal arc welding is classified under the process of...
A] electric resistance welding
B] special welding
C] electric arc welding
D] electro gas welding

79] How to specify the size of an electrode holder?
A] by its weight
B] by its shape
C] by its current carrying capacity
D] by the metal used for making it

80] The current set for a 3.15mm medium coated mild steel electrode is...
A] 50 to 80 amp
B] 90 to 120 amp
C] 120 to 150 amp
D] 150 to 170 amp

81] Which method of cleaning you will use to remove oil, grease and paint from the surface of the metals to be welded?

A] filing
B] wire brushing
C] washing with cold water
D] using solvents of diluted hydrochloric acid

82] In the electrode coding ER4211, the third digit of the number 4211 indicates....
A] welding current and voltage condition
B] elongation and impact properties
C] tensile strength of the joint
D] welding position

83] A long arc is used in...
A] welding with a low hydrogen electrode
B] horizontal position
C] plug or slot welding
D] cast iron welding

84] If the travel speed of electrode is high, which type of weld defect you will get on a T fillet joint?
A] overlap
B] slag inclusion
C] excessive reinforcement
D] lack of root penetration

85] Which weld defect occurs on a lap fillet joint due to improper weaving of the electrode in the covering/final run?
A] crack
B] undercut
C] lack of fusion
D] edge of plate melted off

86] A lap fillet weld has uneven bead height] What is the cause for this defect?
A] use of high current
B] low welding travel speed
C] use of wrist movement for the electrode weaving
D] high welding travel speed

87] The coating factor used to make medium coated electrode is...
A] 1.25 to 3
B] 1.4 to 1.5
C] 1.6 to 2.2
D] above 2.2

88] Which type of coated electrodes are used for general purpose welding and for training purposes in ITIs?
A] basic coated
B] iron powder
C] cellulosic
D] <u>rutile</u>

89] Maintaining a key hole and use of proper root gap in a single V butt joint will ensure...
A] reducing the arc blow effect
B] faster metal deposition
C] <u>proper root penetration</u>
D] proper reinforcement

90] At what angle the electrode is to be held with the bottom surface of the joint in horizontal position?
A] 60° to 70°
B] <u>70° to 80°</u>
C] 80° to 90°
D] 90° to 100°

Q 2) At constant pressure, volume varies as the temperature of the gas. This is statement of .....
1) Boyle s Law
2) <u>Charles Law</u>
3) Joule-Thompson Effect
4) Dalton s Law

Q 3) One ton of refrigeration = ...
1) 45.5 kcal min.
2) <u>50.4 kcal min.</u>
3) 44.5 kcal min.
4) 66.5 kcal min

Q 4) The amount of heat required to raise the temperature of a unit mass of a substance through 1 degree C is called ....
1) <u>Specific heat</u>
2) Sensible heat
3) Latent heat
4) Superheat

Q 5) If the relative humidity of air is 100%, the rate of evaporation will be .....
1) High

2) Medium
3) Low
4) Zero

Q 6) Capillary tube is a device which ....
1) Removes heat carried by the refrigerant
2) Meters the refrigerant
3) Acts as a reservoir for excess liquid refrigerant
4) Pumps the refrigeerant

Q 7) The heart of the refrigeration system is ....
1) Liquid receiver
2) Thermostat
3) Compressor
4) Evaporator

Q 8) Drier used to remove the moisture contents from the liquid refrigerant is charged with ......
1) Silica gel
2) Calcium carbide
3) Clay absorber
4) Ethylene absorber

Q 9) Which of these is not a brine
1) Sodium chloride
2) Calcium chloride
3) Ethylene glycol
4) None of the above

Q 10) A micrometer has a positive error of 0.02 mm. If it reads 25.41 mm, correct reading is .....
1) 25.39 mm
2) 25.37 mm
3) 25.43 mm
4) 25.45 mm

Q 12) Thickness of sheet metal is indicated by a series of numbers called ....
1) Standard size
2) Number size
3) Gauge
4) Normal size

Q 13) One of the functions of welding electrode coating is to ....
1) Increase welding current

2) <u>Stabilize the arc</u>
3) Prevent rusting
4) Control arc temperature

Q 15) The butter compartment of a domestic refrigerator is normally located ......
1) At the top of the cabinet
2) At the bottom of the cabinet
3) At the central height
4) <u>In the door</u>

Q 16) Evaporation process takes place in the evaporator, because of which .....
1) Heat gets added
2) <u>Heat is removed</u>
3) Pressure increases
4) Pressure decreases

Q 17) Snip is a ....
1) Measuring tool
2) Marking tool
3) <u>Cutting tool</u>
4) Supporting tool

Q 18) The unit of frequency is ....
1) Mho
2) Coulomb
3) <u>Hertz</u>
4) Tesla

Q 19) The compressor used in refrigerator is ....
1) <u>Hermetically sealed reciprocating compressor</u>
2) Semi-hermetically sealed reciprocating compressor
3) Open type compressor
4) Centrifugal compressor

Q 20) Domestic refrigerator works on ....
1) <u>Vapour compression cycle</u>
2) Vapour absorption cycle
3) Otto cycle
4) Vapour compression or vapour absorption cycle

Q 21) Which is more efficient - water cooled or air cooled condenser
1) Air cooled
2) <u>Water cooled</u>

3) Both are equally efficient
4) Any one can be more efficient than the other

Q 22) This is NOT a desirable property of insulating material.
1) Resistance to water
2) High thermal conductivity
3) Non-flammable
4) Light in weight

Q 23) One of the complaints against use of window air conditioner is that it is ....
1) Expensive
2) Difficult to install
3) Difficult to maintain
4) Noisy

Q 24) Which of these is NOT a part of outside unit of a split air conditioner
1) Evaporator coil
2) Condenser coil
3) Compressor
4) Expansion coil

Q 25) In a refrigeration cycle, heat is rejected by refrigerant at ....
1) Condenser
2) Evaporator
3) Compressor
4) Expansion valve

Q 26) Which of these is a semi-conductor
1) Gold
2) Lead
3) Silicon
4) Plastic

Q 27) The cooling effect in a cooling tower can be increased by ....
1) Increasing velocity of air over wet surface
2) Lowering barometric pressure
3) Reducing humidity of air
4) All of the above

Q 28) CRO gives ....
1) Actual representation
2) Visual representation

3) Approximate representation
4) Incorrect representation
Q 29) Integrated circuits are normally made of ....
1) <u>Silicon</u>
2) Germanium
3) Copper
4) Aluminium
Q 30) The active components in an IC are ....
1) Resistors
2) Capacitors
3) <u>Transistors and diodes</u>
4) None of the above
Q 31) Temporary hardness of water is removed by ....
1) Filtering
2) <u>Boiling</u>
3) Chemical treatment
4) None of the above
Q 32) Natural draft cooling towers are mainly used in ....
1) Steel plants
2) <u>Power stations</u>
3) Fertilizer plants
4) Aluminium manufacturing plants
Q 33) What is used in pre-treatment of water to remove large objects
1) Bacteria
2) Oil and grease
3) Air
4) <u>Screen</u>
Q 34) In the evaporator the refrigerant enters at ....
1) <u>Very low pressure</u>
2) Low pressure
3) Medium pressure
4) High pressure
Q 35) The type of evaporator used in large refrigeration and central air conditioning systems is
1) <u>Shell and tube evaporator</u>
2) Finned evaporator
3) Plate surface evaporator
4) Bare tube evaporator

Q 36) Why are ice cans made tapered in height
1) To reduce weight
2) <u>To facilitate dumping</u>
3) To improve appearance
4) To make fabrication easier

Q 37) The instrument used to measure relative humidity is ....
1) Barometer
2) <u>Psychrometer</u>
3) Manometer
4) Pressure gauge

Q 38) Pressure on the high pressure side of a mechanical refrigeration unit is called
1) Suction pressure
2) <u>Discharge or head pressure</u>
3) Differential pressure _
4) Absolute pressure _

Q 42) Dry bulb temperature (DBT) is the actual temperature of ....
1) <u>Moist air</u>
2) Dry air
3) Dry ice
4) Saturated air

Q 43) AHU stands for ....
1) <u>Air Handling Unit</u>
2) Air Heating Unit
3) Air Humidifying Unit
4) None of these

Q 44) Refrigeration is used in medical industry for_____
1) <u>storing blood</u>
2) refining petroleum
3) production of ice
4) production of rocket fuel

Q 46) Which of the following tools is used to open and close the service valve
1) <u>Cylindrical valve key</u>
2) Pinching Tool
3) Punch set
4) Swagging Tool

Q 47) _____ is a cutting tool used to make the metal surface smooth.
1) <u>File</u>
2) Hacksaw
3) Scriber
4) Trammel

Q 48) Which of these is used to make deep holes in the wood
1) <u>Gimlet</u>
2) Stake
3) Snap
4) Mallet

Q 49) Which of the following device measures electric current in a circuit
1) <u>Ammeter</u>
2) Wattmeter
3) Voltmeter
4) Watt-hour meter

Q 50) _____ is not an insulator.
1) <u>Eureka</u>
2) Asbestos
3) Ebonite
4) Glass

Q 51) The unit of Impedance is_____.
1) <u>Ohm</u>
2) Ohm-metre
3) Henry
4) Farad

Q 52) Universal A.C. motor provides _____ torque and operates at _____ speed.
1) <u>high, high</u>
2) high, low
3) low, high
4) low, low

Q 53) At which of the following places, slip ring motors are used 1. planer 2. crane 3. lathe 4. grinder slotter Select the correct answer from the codes given below.
1) <u>1,2</u>
2) 2,3

3) 1,2,3
4) 2,4

Q 54) _____ is primarily used in compressor.
1) <u>Capacitor start capacitor run motor</u>
2) Hysteresis motor
3) Shaded pole induction motor
4) Repulsion motor _

Q 55) P-type semiconductor cannot be made by adding _____ with Germanium.
1) <u>Arsenic</u>
2) Indium
3) Gallium
4) Boron

Q 56) Laser diode finds its application in_____
1) <u>fibre amplifier</u>
2) television receiver
3) remote controls
4) photo conductors

Q 58) Which of these is used as a charger in the machine used for refrigeration
1) <u>Refrigerant adapter</u>
2) Charging meter
3) Vaccum pump
4) Compressor oil charging pump

Q 59) In Vapour Absorption refrigeration, _____ is used for refrigeration.
1) <u>Heat energy</u>
2) Mechanical energy
3) Potential energy
4) Chemical energy

Q 61) Compressors cannot be classified a_____ according to the method of compression.
1) <u>Multi stage compressor</u>
2) Reciprocating compressor
3) Rotating compressor
4) Centrifugal compressor

Q 62) The efficiency of centrifugal compressors as compared to that of reciprocating compressors is

1) <u>high</u>
2) low
3) equal
4) low or equal

Q 63) Which of the following compressors are primarily considered as the most appropriate for refrigerant fluid
1) <u>Scroll compressor</u>
2) Hermetically sealed compressor
3) Swash plate compressor
4) Wobble plate compressor

Q 64) Wet compression_____ the compressor efficiency.
1) increases
2) <u>decreases</u>
3) halves
4) has no effect on

Q 65) Water cooled condensers have _____ heat transfer rate as compared to air cooled condensers.
1) <u>high</u>
2) low
3) equal
4) low or equal

Q 66) Which of these is a tank shaped device used for storing liquid refrigerant in refrigeration
1) <u>Liquid receiver</u>
2) Condenser
3) Compressor oil charging pump
4) Evaporator

Q 67) The compressor compresses the refrigerant to high pressure to_____
1) <u>increase the temperature</u>
2) heat the refrigerant
3) decrease the temperature
4) condense the refrigerant

Q 68) Both air and water are used as cooling medium in _____ condenser.
1) <u>evaporative</u>
2) shell and tube
3) shell and coil

4) air cooled

Q 69) Plate surface evaporators are not used in_____
1) food processing industry
2) ice-cream cabinet -
3) domestic refrigerator
4) freezer

Q 70) In order to prevent the quantity of liquid refrigerant present in the refrigerant obtained from evaporator from entering into the condenser, _____ is connected between evaporator and compressor.
1) accumulator
2) superheater
3) bottle cooler
4) water cooler

Q 71) In reverse cycle defrosting, evaporator works like a_____.
1) Condenser
2) evaporator itself
3) expansion valve
4) accumulator

Q 72) Where do the automatic expansion valves find their application
1) In domestic refrigerator
2) In food processing units
3) In air conditioners
4) In ice-cream plants

Q 73) Change of pressure of capillary tube is _____ the diameter of capillary tube.
1) directly proportional to
2) inversely proportional to
3) directly proportional to the square of
4) inversely proportional to the square of

Q 74) Which of the following removes moisture from refrigerant in an air-conditioning system
1) Drier
2) expansion valve
3) Condenser
4) capillary tube

Q 75) Which of these is a secondary refrigerant
1) Brine
2) Ammonia

3) Freon
4) Methyl chloride

Q 76) Chemical formula of Freon-12 is_____.
1) <u>CCl2F2</u>
2) CF2
3) CCl2
4) CCl4

Q 77) The refrigerant symbol for Methane (CH4) is_____
1) <u>R-50</u>
2) R-14
3) R-11
4) R-240

Q 78) _____ is not an anti-freeze substance. _____
1) <u>Methylene Chloride</u>
2) Methyl Alcohol
3) Ethylene Glycol
4) Glycerine

Q 79) Which of these thermal insulations used in refrigeration has highest density
1) <u>Calcium silicate</u>
2) Cotton
3) Granulate
4) Wool

Q 80) _____ is an outlet grill designed to guide the direction of air in the duct system.
1) <u>diffuser</u>
2) ejector
3) register
4) converter

Q 81) The free wheel used in automotive vehicles is also known as _____
1) <u>over running clutch</u>
2) under running cluth
3) magnetic clutch
4) automatic clutch

Q 82) In a car A.C., compressor is connected with the _____.
1) <u>engine</u>
2) clutch

3) chasis
4) wheels

Q 83) If the split A.C. is giving insufficient air cooling, then which of the given is a possible reason
1) <u>air filter is dirty</u>
2) timer setting is changed
3) main supply is defective
4) outer temperature is low

Q 84) _____ measures pressure and vaccum in an air conditioning system.
1) <u>Compound gauge</u>
2) Vaccum gauge
3) Tachometer
4) Pressure gauge

Q 85) In a window air conditioner, _____ evaporator is used.
1) <u>fin type</u>
2) coil type
3) spiral
4) duct-type

Q 86) In case of damage in compressor of a refrigeration system and blockage of dryer etc., _____ is done.
1) <u>retrofitting</u>
2) suction
3) insulation
4) expansion

Q 87) Which of these amounts to the difference between moist temperature and real liquid refrigerant temperature
1) <u>Sub-cooling</u>
2) Superheating
3) Evaporation
4) Condensation

Q 88) Expansion valve controls the _____ in the evaporator.
1) <u>amount of refrigerant</u>
2) temperature of system
3) temperature of refrigerant
4) pressure of system

Q 89) The part of a screw compressor to which the rotor is attached is called_____.
1) <u>housing</u>
2) driver
3) discharge port
4) casing

Q 90) What happens to the volumetric efficiency during a pressure drop in the compressor
1) <u>It increases</u>
2) It decreases
3) It remains unchanged
4) It may increase or decrease

Q 91) What are the applications of commercial compressor 1. water coolers 2. cold storage 3. ice cube machine Out of the above options, which of these is are correct
1) <u>1,2,3</u>
2) 2,3
3) 1,3
4) 1,2

Q 92) Stuck-up fault in a compressor means_____.
1) <u>compressor is working tightly</u>
2) compressor is making noise
3) there is friction in compressor
4) compressor is not starting

Q 93) Which of the following is used to make the natural air enter the closed cooling tower
1) <u>Fan</u>
2) Blower _
3) Cooler
4) Air conditioner

Q 94) _____are attached in a Natural draft cooling tower to control the flow of air.
1) <u>Louvres</u>
2) Spray nozzles
3) Header
4) Valve

Q 95) Operating cost of mechanical draft cooling towers are compared to natural draft is____

1) <u>high</u>
2) low
3) equal
4) incomparable

Q 96) Wet bulb temperature is _____ the cooling tower capacity.
1) <u>inversely proportional</u>
2) directly proportional
3) inversely propotional to the square of
4) directly proportional to the square of

Q 97) Sludge is usually formed due to_____.
1) <u>Calcium Chloride</u>
2) Zinc Chloride
3) Hydrochloric acid
4) Sulphuric acid

Q 98) Which of these is not an external treatment given to scale formation
1) <u>Colloidal treatment</u>
2) Ion exchange process
3) Zeolite process
4) Soda lime process

Q 99) In electric treatment of water, sealed glass bulbs filled with_____ vapours are placed in the system in order to block the scale formation process.
2) <u>sodium</u>
3) helium
4) argon

Q 101) The amount of refrigerant passed by the valve is_____ the amount of refrigerant vapourized by the evaporator.
1) <u>equal to</u>
2) half
3) one-fourth
4) double

Q 102) _____ is used as an expansion valve in a flooded evaporator.
1) <u>Float valve</u>
2) Thermostatic valve
3) Capillary tube

4) Orifice control valve

Q 103) Brine chiller is similar to_____ of a vapour compression refrigeration system.
1) <u>evaporator</u>
2) Condenser
3) compressor
4) Capillary tube

Q 104) Condenser capacity is measured in_____
1) <u>kW</u>
2) kV
3) kVA
4) kA

Q 105) The capacity of condenser is not a function of_____
1) <u>volume of refrigerant</u>
2) surface area of condenser
3) overall heat transfer coefficient
4) temperature difference between refrigerant and condenser medium

Q 106) Cooling medium in Evaporative condenser is_____
1) <u>both air and water</u>
2) brine
3) air only
4) water only

Q 107) Wet bulb temperature is a measure of_____.
1) <u>absolute humidity</u>
2) absolute pressure
3) relative humidity
4) specific heat

Q 108) The temperature at which moisture in the air starts condensing is called_____.
1) <u>dew point temperature</u>
2) wet bulb temperature
3) dry bulb temperature
4) dew point depression

Q 109) _____ duct system is commonly used to obtain an efficient duct using friction method.
1) <u>Rectangular</u>
2) Square
3) Circular

4) Triangular

Q 110) Ducting done in large offices using_____type distribution.
1) <u>Ceiling panel</u>
2) Upward
3) Pan
4) Wall

Q 111) Which of these is NOT a probable reason for improper working of condenser unit
1) <u>Temperature is not set</u>
2) Condenser has become dirty
3) Air does not flow
4) Spray nozzle is closed

Q 112) The part of a duct used for joining two duct lines at right angle is called_____
1) <u>stack elbow</u>
2) outlet port
3) duct joint
4) tee joint

Q 113) In a direct expansion system, which of these is found in Plant room
2) <u>Air filter</u>
3) evaporator
4) Return air duct

Q 114) _____ is a device by which cool, clean and humid air can be obtained.
1) <u>Air washer</u>
2) Fan coil
3) Relief valve
4) Spray Nozzle

Q 115) _____ is installed in the circuit for usage of electromechanical controls.
1) <u>Relay</u>
2) Meggar
3) Circuit Breaker
4) Fuse

Q 116) H stands for_____in HVAC systems.
1) <u>Heating</u>

2) Healing
3) Honning
4) Heavy

Q 117) _____coil is fitted in HVAC system.
1) Both heating and cooling
2) Only heating
3) Only cooling
4) condensation

Q 118) In a car A.C., condenser is fitted near_____
1) radiator
2) rear wheel
3) crankcase
4) magnetic clutch

Q 119) Car A.C. operates at maximum efficiency when running at _____
1) high speed
2) zero speed
3) low speed
4) zero load

Q 120) In order to_____ , dye is added to car A.C. system.
1) identify the gas leak
2) lubricate the engine
3) increase efficiency
4) increase speed

Q 121) Which of the following does not affects heat load calculation in an A.C. plant
1) Outer temperature
2) Relative humidity
3) Dew point _
4) Moisture

Q 122) _____in the condenser maintains the required level of water.
1) Flow switch
2) Overload circuit
3) Cut-out switch -
4) Strainer

Q 123) The application of fans and blowers in central A.C. plant is_____
1) circulation of air
2) heating
3) cooling
4) chilling

Q 124) The nature of air in summer air conditioning is_____
1) heated and humidified
2) heated and dehumidified
3) cooled and humidified
4) cooled and dehumidified

Q 125) If a deep freezer does not give enough cooling, then it must be due to_____
1) continuous opening of door
2) no power supply
3) high external pressure
4) high external temperature

Q 126) Which of these is not a part of Ice cream plant
1) Ice bin
2) Heat exchanger
3) Pasteurizer
4) Homogenizer

Q 127) On switching on the _____, ice produced due to excess cooling starts melting
1) Defrost switch
2) Overload relay
3) Flow switch
4) Thermostat

Q 128) Carrot can be stored for 3 months at a temperature of _____
1) 2 °C
2) 8 °C
3) 5 °C
4) 10 °C

Q 129) The unit of cold storage capacity is_____.
1) tonne
2) kilogram
3) cubic metre

4) degree kelvin

INDUSTRIAL TRAINING INSTITUTE
Monthly Test-1, Marks- 20, Date:- _____
(Every Question Carry Two Marks)

1] Which one is a workshop safety?
A] Keep shop floor clean and free from grease, oil or other slippery materials
B] Stop the machine before changing the speed
C] Don't use cracked or chipped tools
D] Don't try to stop a running machine with hand

2] In Personal Protect Equipment (PPE) HELMET is used to
A] protect head
B] Protect eyes
C] Protect hands
D] Protect ears

3] Which of the following belongs to general safety?
A Have a worker in good attitude
B] The work clean and clear
C] Concentrate on your work
D] Keep the floor and gangways clean and clear

4] While grinding, which is used to protect the eyes?
A] Dark green glass
B] Mask
C] Sun glasses
D] Safety goggles

5] Which of the following is done for machine safety?
A] Check the oil level before starting the machine
B] Do things in a methodical way
C] Keep the floor and gangways clean and clear
D] Don't use dies and scarves

6] In Personal Protect Equipment (PPE), 'sleeves' is used to protect ----------
A] Face
B] Eyes
C] Ears
D] Hands

7] ABC stands for --------------

A] Automatic Breathing Control
B] Automatic Blood Control
C] Airway Breathing Circulation
D] Automatic Blood Circulation
9] To put off"Class B" fire, the types of fire extinguisher used is ....
A] dry power
B] Carbon dioxide
C] Jet of water
D] Foam type
10] Which type of fire extinguisher is used to put off general fire?
A] Water type Extinguisher
B] Foam type Extinguisher
C] Dry chemical powder Extinguisher
D] Carbon dioxide (C02] Extinguisher
11] In case of bleeding, take treatment Of
D] cold 3" and rest
A] spray cold water
B] Bandage immediately -----.
B] Enquire about the accident thought treatment

INDUSTRIAL TRAINING INSTITUTE
Monthly Test-2, Marks- 20, Date:- _____
(Every Question Carry Two Marks)

20] The size of the dividers are specified by the -----------
A] Total length of legs
B] Distance between the points when fully opened
C] Length of legs without points
D] distance between the pivot and the point
21] The instrument used to mark parallel lines, parallel to the datum edge is -
A] jenny caliper
B] Divider
C] Outside calliper
D] Inside calliper
22] Which one of the following is an indirect measuring tool?
A] Outside caliper
B] Vernier calliper
C] Steel rule
D] Outside micrometer

23] For cutting thin tubing, the most suitable pitch of the hacksaw blade is...
A] 1.8mm
B] 1.4mm
C] 1mm
D] 0.8mm

24] For cutting solid brass, the most suitable pitch of the hacksaw blade is...
A] 1.8mm
B] 1.4mm
C] 1mm
D] 0.8mm

25] A new hacksaw blade after a few strokes becomes loose because of the...
A] Stretching of the blade
B] Wing-nut threads being worn out
C] Wrong pitch of the blade
D] Improper selection of the set of saws.

26] While cutting small diameter pipes, it is advisable to watch regularly and ensure that...
A] The cut is along the curved line
B] More saw teeth are in contract
C] The work is not overheated
D] Proper balancing of hacksaw is maintained

27] The vice clamps are used to...
A] Protect hard jaws
B] Clamp the work pieces rigidly
C] Protect the finished surfaces
D] Prevent the movable jaw being filed

28] The reference surface during marking is provided by the...
A] Surface gauge
B] Workpiece
C] Drawing of the work
D] Marking table surface

29] The size of an engineer's vice is specified by the...
A] Length of the movable jaw
B] Width of the jaws
C] Height of the vice

D] Maximum opening of the jaws

INDUSTRIAL TRAINING INSTITUTE
Monthly Test-3, Marks- 20, Date:- _____
(Every Question Carry Two Marks)

61] in a metric micrometer, a complete revolution of thimble advances -----------

A] 0.01 mm
B] 0.25 mm
C] 0.50 mm
D] 1.00mm

62] Ratchet Stop in the micrometer helps to ------------
A] Control the pressure
B] lock the spindle
C] Adjust the zero error
D] Hold the work piece

63] 1000 micron means ------------
A] 1 mm
B] 1 m
C] 1000 mm
D] 10 cm

64] What is the zero reading of a 50-75 mm outside micrometer?
A] 0.000 mm
B] 0.01 mm
C] 25.00 mm
D] 50.00 mm

65] The value of the smallest division on sleeve of a metric outside micrometer is -----
A] 0.50 mm
B] 1.00 mm
C] 1.50 mm
D] 2.00 mm

66] Ratchet stop in the micrometer helps to ---------
A] control the pressure
B] Lock the spindle
C] Adjust the zero error
D] Hold the work piece

67] Least count of depth micrometer is
A] 0.5 mm

B] 0.2 mm
C] 0.001 mm
D] 0.01 mm

68] The least count of vernier calliper is (main scale = 49 division, vernier scale = 50 division]
A] 0.1 mm
B] 0.01 mm
C] 0.001 mm
D] 0.02 mm

69] The type of measurement made by using a Vernier Calliper is -------
A] Direct measurement
B] Indirect measurement
C] 90"] (a] 81 (b]
D] None of these

76] The taper shank drills are held on the machine by means of...
A] Chucks
B] Sleeves
C] Drift
D] Vice

INDUSTRIAL TRAINING INSTITUTE
Monthly Test-4, Marks- 20, Date:- _____
(Every Question Carry Two Marks)

Q 41. A piece of material which is cut to the exact size and shape to form the desired object is called _____
A). Pattern
B). Templates
C). Stretchout
D). Development

Q 42. The term_____ refers to the sizes of flat piece of metal before it is formed into shape.
A). Stretchout
B). Free hand sketch
C). Actual size
D). Development of surface

Q 43. Which of the following is not possible with the parallel line method
A). Pyramid
B). Cube

C). Prism
D). Cylinder

Q 44. Which of the following is a method of dividing the surface of the object in traingles
A). Triangulation method
B). Geometrical construction methods
C). Parallel line method
D). Radial line method

Q 45. Which type of punches have hollow cross-section
A). Hollow punch
B). Solid punch
C). Number punch
D). Letter punch

Q 46. Which type of rivet is used in heavy structural work
A). Pan head rivet
B). Snap head rivet
C). Counter sunk rivet
D). Conical head rivet

Q 47. Identify the rivet as shown in figure
A). Pan head
B). Countersunk head
C). Snap head
D). Mushroom head

Q 48. The government clip are sometimes also called_____
A). Cup or Pocket Clip
B). Nailing Clip
C). Drive Clip
D). S-Clip

Q 49. Which clip is generally used for connecting cross seams on ducts
A). Drive Clip
B). S-Clip
C). Government Clip
D). Nailing Clip

Q 50. Which of the following solder is the alloy of copper, tin, silver, zinc, cadmium and phosphorus
A). Hard solders
B). Soft solders
C). Medium solders

D). Zinc solders

INDUSTRIAL TRAINING INSTITUTE
Monthly Test-5, Marks- 20, Date:- _____
(Every Question Carry Two Marks)

100] Heat developed in a conductor is proportional to the...
A] square of the power
B] square of the resistance
C] square of the current
D] square of the time

101] Out of the four metal/alloys given below, one has almost no change in resistance for temperature change...
A] nickel
B] nichrome
C] platinum
D] manganin

102] A material that is slightly repelled by a magnet is called ...
A] magnetic
B] paramagnetic
C] diamagnetic
D] ferromagnetic

103] A material that can be magnetized only very slightly is called...
A] magnetic
B] paramagnetic
C] diamagnetic
D] ferromagnetic

104] Substances that can be magnetized easily and make very strong magnets are called...
A] ferromagnetic
B] diamagnetic
C] paramagnetic
D] permanent magnetic

105] A substance that has a high retentivity can be used for the manufacture of...
A] electromagnets
B] permanent magnets
C] temporary magnets
D] paramagnets

106] A substance that has low retentivity can be used for the manufacture of...
A] electromagnets
B] permanent magnets
C] bar magnets
D] paramagnets

107] The symbol for inductance is...
A] H
B] I
C] L
D] X

108] Tube lamp choke is the best example of...
A] open circuited
B] short circuited
C] grounded
D] connected to the neutral line

109] The initial function of a choke in a tube light circuit is to...
A] limit the starting current
B] induce high voltage
C] heat up the filament
D] limit the current after starting

INDUSTRIAL TRAINING INSTITUTE
Monthly Test-6, Marks- 20, Date:- _____
(Every Question Carry Two Marks)

121] A capacitor is connected across a 200 volt AC line, its minimum voltage rating should be...
A] 100 volts
B] 200 Volts
C] 300 volts
D] 400 volts

122] when testing a capacitor with an ohmmeter, the meter indicates some resistance] The capacitor under test is...
A] leaky
B] open
C] good
D] short

123] The total capacitance of a 40 micro farad capacitor connected in series with an 80 micro farad capacitor is...

A] 26.7 micro farad
B] 40 micro farad
C] 60.6 micro farad
D] 120 micro farad

124] For obtaining 1 micro farad capacitor from 3 nos] of 3 micro farad capacitors we have to connect...
A] all in parallel
B] all in series
C] 2 series and one in parallel
D] none of the above

125] In an AC series circuit having R and C the current flowing through the capacitor will be...
A] lagging the voltage
B] leading the voltage
C] in phase with the voltage
D] none of the above

126] If the frequency of the supply is increased in the R-C series circuit the capacitive reactance will be
A] reduced
B] increased
C] having no effect
D] none of the above

127] Power companies are interested in improving the power factor to
A] reduce line current
B] increase motor efficiency
C] increase volt-amperes
D] decrease power

128] A capacitor increases the power factor value of an AC motor load when it is connected...
A] in series with the motor
B] in series with the starter
C] in parallel with the motor
D] in series with the main winding

129] Normally, the power factor of an incandescent lighting circuit is..
A] 0
B] 0.5
C] 0.707
D] 1.0

130] When resistance alone is used to determine current in an RLC series circuit, the circuit is...
A] an inductive circuit
B] a capacitive circuit
C] a combination circuit
D] a resonant circuit

INDUSTRIAL TRAINING INSTITUTE
Monthly Test-7, Marks- 20, Date:- _____
(Every Question Carry Two Marks)

150] Two wattmeters can be used to measure 3-hase power in a 3-phase, 3 wire system with...
A] balanced load
B] unbalanced load
C] balanced as well as unbalanced load
D] out of balanced load

151] A single wattmeter can be used to measure power in a 3-phase system only when the load is..
A] balanaced
B] unbalanced
C] balanced as well as unbalanced load
D] constant

152] The force producing movement of the pointer in an indicating instrument is called as...
A] deflecting force
B] controlling force
C] damping force
D] distracting force

153] A permanent magnet moving coil instrument will read...
A] only AC quantities
B] only DC quantities
C] both AC and DC quantities
D] pulsating quantities

154] An instrument using gravity control will read correctly if used in..
A] vertical position only
B] horizontal position only
C] inclined position only
D] any position

155] Which one of the following damping methods is used in permanent magnet moving coil instrument?
A] air damping
B] fluid damping
C] spring damping
D] eddy current damping

156] Moving coil instrument works on the effect of...
A] chemical effect
B] heating effect
C] electrostatic effect
D] electromagnetic effect

157] The meter installed at your house to measure electrical energy is an example of...
A] indication type instrument
B] recording type instrument
C] indicating as well as recording type instrument
D] integrating type instrument

158].Which of the following material is preferred for permanent magnet?
A] alnico
B] y-alloy
C] silicon steel

1. A transistor has ....
A] one pn junction
B] two pn junctions
C] three pn junctions
D] four pn junctions

INDUSTRIAL TRAINING INSTITUTE
Monthly Test-8, Marks- 20, Date:- _____
(Every Question Carry Two Marks)

40] The angle of below pipe to the line of weld in leftward welding technique is...
A] 40 to 50°
B] 50 to 60°
C] 60 to 70°
D] 70 to 80°

41] The pressure of acetylene gas for gas cutting a 10mm M.S plate is...
A] 0.15 kgf/cm2

B] 0.5 kgf/cm2
C] 1.0 kgf/cm2
D] 1.5 kgf/cm2

42] What size of the cutting nozzle you will select for cutting 10mm thick mild steel?
A] 0.8 mm
B] 1.2 mm
C] 1.6 mm
D] 2.0 mm

43] The angle of filler rod in case of rightward welding technique is...
A] 10 to 20°
B] 20 to 30°
C] 30 to 40°
D] 40 to 50°

44] One of the advantages of the high pressure system of gas welding is...
A] it is cheaper
B] it is portable
C] it is less dangerous
D] it does not require a skilled welder

45] Soldering of M.S sheets takes place at a temperature of...
A] 150°C
B] 250°C
C] 400°C
D] 850°C

46] Forge welding is classified as...
A] fusion welding without pressure
B] fusion welding with pressure
C] non-fusion welding without pressure
D] no-fusion welding with pressure

47] The function of a gas regulator is...
A] get different types of flames
B] mix the gases in the required proportion
C] change the volume of gas flowing to the blow pipe
D] set the working pressure

48] For welding a lap fillet joint in vertical position by gas what should be the angle of below pipe to the line of weld?
A] 30° to 40°

B] 45° to 50°
C] 60° to 70°
D] 75° to 80°

49] Name the defect, in which the weld metal is flowing on to the surface of the base metal without fusing it
A] crater
B] overlap
C] lack of fusion
D] excessive convexity

INDUSTRIAL TRAINING INSTITUTE
Monthly Test-9, Marks- 20, Date:- _____
(Every Question Carry Two Marks)

71] Nozzle size used for welding a 2 mm thick stainless steel sheet as a butt joint is...
A] 2
B] 3
C] 5
D] 7

72] What is the value of preheating temperature for gas welding of aluminium?
A] 100 to 120°C
B] 150 to 180°C
C] 180 to 200°C
D] 210 to 250°C

73] In soldering operation the base metal is...
A] not heated
B] heated to 200°C
C] heated to 650°C
D] heated to red hot condition

74] For welding dissimilar metals, the following property of both the metals should not have wide variations
A] ductility
B] tensile strength
C] thermal expansion
D] wear resistance

75] Name the flux used for brazing of M.S] sheets
A] hydrochloric acid

B] zinc chloride
C] tallow resin
D] borax

76] In progressive gouging to what angle the gouging torch angle is reduced from the starting angle of 30°?

A] 20 to 25°
B] 15 to 20°
C] 10 to 15°
D] 5 to 10°

77] The thermit mixture used in thermit welding can be ignited with an initial temperature of..

A] 1500°C
B] 1200°C
C] 1000°C
D] 500°C

78] Shielded metal arc welding is classified under the process of...

A] electric resistance welding
B] special welding
C] electric arc welding
D] electro gas welding

79] How to specify the size of an electrode holder?

A] by its weight
B] by its shape
C] by its current carrying capacity
D] by the metal used for making it

80] The current set for a 3.15mm medium coated mild steel electrode is...

A] 50 to 80 amp
B] 90 to 120 amp
C] 120 to 150 amp
D] 150 to 170 amp

INDUSTRIAL TRAINING INSTITUTE
Monthly Test-10, Marks- 20, Date:- _____
(Every Question Carry Two Marks)

Q 2) At constant pressure, volume varies as the temperature of the gas. This is statement of .....

1) Boyle s Law

2) Charles Law
3) Joule-Thompson Effect
4) Dalton s Law
Q 3) One ton of refrigeration = ...
1) 45.5 kcal min.
2) 50.4 kcal min.
3) 44.5 kcal min.
4) 66.5 kcal min
Q 4) The amount of heat required to raise the temperature of a unit mass of a substance through 1 degree C is called ....
1) Specific heat
2) Sensible heat
3) Latent heat
4) Superheat
Q 5) If the relative humidity of air is 100%, the rate of evaporation will be .....
1) High
2) Medium
3) Low
4) Zero
Q 6) Capillary tube is a device which ....
1) Removes heat carried by the refrigerant
2) Meters the refrigerant
3) Acts as a reservoir for excess liquid refrigerant
4) Pumps the refrigeerant
Q 7) The heart of the refrigeration system is ....
1) Liquid receiver
2) Thermostat
3) Compressor
4) Evaporator
Q 8) Drier used to remove the moisture contents from the liquid refrigerant is charged with ......
1) Silica gel
2) Calcium carbide
3) Clay absorber
4) Ethylene absorber
Q 9) Which of these is not a brine
1) Sodium chloride

2) Calcium chloride
3) Ethylene glycol
4) None of the above

Q 10) A micrometer has a positive error of 0.02 mm. If it reads 25.41 mm, correct reading is .....

1) 25.39 mm
2) 25.37 mm
3) 25.43 mm
4) 25.45 mm

Q 12) Thickness of sheet metal is indicated by a series of numbers called ....

1) Standard size
2) Number size
3) Gauge
4) Normal size

INDUSTRIAL TRAINING INSTITUTE
Monthly Test-11, Marks- 20, Date:- _____
(Every Question Carry Two Marks)

Q 10) A micrometer has a positive error of 0.02 mm. If it reads 25.41 mm, correct reading is .....

1) 25.39 mm
2) 25.37 mm
3) 25.43 mm
4) 25.45 mm

Q 12) Thickness of sheet metal is indicated by a series of numbers called ....

1) Standard size
2) Number size
3) Gauge
4) Normal size

Q 13) One of the functions of welding electrode coating is to ....

1) Increase welding current
2) Stabilize the arc
3) Prevent rusting
4) Control arc temperature

Q 15) The butter compartment of a domestic refrigerator is normally located ......

1) At the top of the cabinet

2) At the bottom of the cabinet
3) At the central height
4) In the door

Q 16) Evaporation process takes place in the evaporator, because of which .....
1) Heat gets added
2) Heat is removed
3) Pressure increases
4) Pressure decreases

Q 17) Snip is a ....
1) Measuring tool
2) Marking tool
3) Cutting tool
4) Supporting tool

Q 18) The unit of frequency is ....
1) Mho
2) Coulomb
3) Hertz
4) Tesla

Q 19) The compressor used in refrigerator is ....
1) Hermetically sealed reciprocating compressor
2) Semi-hermetically sealed reciprocating compressor
3) Open type compressor
4) Centrifugal compressor

Q 20) Domestic refrigerator works on ....
1) Vapour compression cycle
2) Vapour absorption cycle
3) Otto cycle
4) Vapour compression or vapour absorption cycle

Q 21) Which is more efficient - water cooled or air cooled condenser
1) Air cooled
2) Water cooled
3) Both are equally efficient
4) Any one can be more efficient than the other

INDUSTRIAL TRAINING INSTITUTE
Monthly Test-12, Marks- 20, Date:-_____
(Every Question Carry Two Marks)

Q 31) Temporary hardness of water is removed by ....

1) Filtering
2) Boiling
3) Chemical treatment
4) None of the above

Q 32) Natural draft cooling towers are mainly used in ....
1) Steel plants
2) Power stations
3) Fertilizer plants
4) Aluminium manufacturing plants

Q 33) What is used in pre-treatment of water to remove large objects
1) Bacteria
2) Oil and grease
3) Air
4) Screen

Q 34) In the evaporator the refrigerant enters at ....
1) Very low pressure
2) Low pressure
3) Medium pressure
4) High pressure

Q 35) The type of evaporator used in large refrigeration and central air conditioning systems is
1) Shell and tube evaporator
2) Finned evaporator
3) Plate surface evaporator
4) Bare tube evaporator

Q 36) Why are ice cans made tapered in height
1) To reduce weight
2) To facilitate dumping
3) To improve appearance
4) To make fabrication easier

Q 37) The instrument used to measure relative humidity is ....
1) Barometer
2) Psychrometer
3) Manometer
4) Pressure gauge

Q 38) Pressure on the high pressure side of a mechanical refrigeration unit is called
1) Suction pressure

2) Discharge or head pressure
3) Differential pressure _
4) Absolute pressure _

Q 42) Dry bulb temperature (DBT) is the actual temperature of ....
1) Moist air
2) Dry air
3) Dry ice
4) Saturated air

Q 43) AHU stands for ....
1) Air Handling Unit
2) Air Heating Unit
3) Air Humidifying Unit
4) None of these

www.ingramcontent.com/pod-product-compliance
Ingram Content Group UK Ltd.
Pitfield, Milton Keynes, MK11 3LW, UK
UKHW040742200825
7484UKWH00033B/608